Zuppa!

Other Books by Margaret and G. Franco Romagnoli

The Romagnolis' Italian Fish Cookbook

The Romagnolis' Table

The Romagnolis' Meatless Cookbook
(reissued as *Carnevale Italiano*)

The New Italian Cooking

The New Romagnolis' Table

Cucina Americana (published in Italy)

Zuppa!

A Tour of the Many Regions of Italy and Their Soups

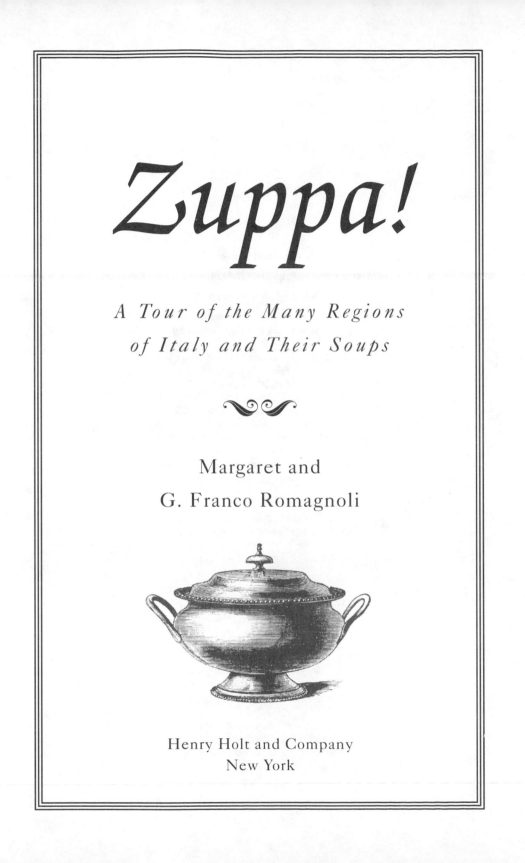

Margaret and
G. Franco Romagnoli

Henry Holt and Company
New York

Henry Holt and Company, Inc.
Publishers since 1866
115 West 18th Street
New York, New York 10011

Henry Holt® is a registered
trademark of Henry Holt and Company, Inc.

Published in Canada by Fitzhenry & Whiteside Ltd.,
195 Allstate Parkway, Markham, Ontario L3R 4T8.

Library of Congress Cataloging-in-Publication Data
Romagnoli, Margaret.
Zuppa!: a tour of the many regions of Italy and
their soups / Margaret and G. Franco Romagnoli.—1st ed.
p.   cm.
Includes index.
1. Soups.   2. Cookery, Italian.   3. Italy—Description and
travel.   I. Romagnoli, G. Franco.   II. Title.
TX757.R726   1996   96-13287
641.8′ 13—dc20   CIP

ISBN 0-8050-3833-7

Henry Holt books are available for special promotions
and premiums. For details contact: Director, Special Markets.

First Edition—1996

A small portion of a few chapters as well as a few fish soup recipes
have been previously published in some food magazines and
in the food section of a newspaper.

Designed by Betty Lew

Printed in the United States of America
All first editions are printed on acid-free paper. ∞

1   3   5   7   9   10   8   6   4   2

For Margherita,

To whom this book, and I, owe so much.

Franco

Contents

Introduction

In the Italian food lexicon, *Zuppa* can be compared to the kettledrum in an orchestra, which has a very important, low and rolling sound with a full range of volume and dynamics. In Italy the word *zuppa* has a larger meaning than the English word *soup*. Soup is understood to be something—vegetables, meat, fish, or fowl—cooked in a broth, with or without thickeners. A real Italian *zuppa* rests its strength on the slices of yesterday's bread that act as carrier and catalyzer of all flavors. It is nourishment for the soul, reminiscent of the warmth and fragrance of the family hearth, of the first food—after a mother's milk—offered to a baby or to an old person as a soothing, comforting meal. *Zuppa* is what people work for, what gives vigor and energy ("Go and get yourself a *zuppa!*" is how fans boo a weak, failing athlete), and what young recruits run to when the bugle urgently blares the mess call:

La zuppa l'è cotta,	(Soup's cooked . . .
La zuppa l'è cotta.	Soup's cooked.
La zuppa l'è pronta . . .	Soup's ready . . .
Venite a mangiar!	Come and get it!)

It is as simple a menu as you can get, but it represents, metaphorically, the whole range of what is nourishing and good.

Until quite recently, in the real, nonmetaphorical sense, most of the time *zuppa* was not only the essence of the meal but the whole meal itself. In what is a basically peasant cuisine (which is where the roots of most Italian cookery rest), what went into the soup is what the land—and hence the larder—had to offer. It all ended up in the boiling kettle to accompany substantial slices of bread.

Today, with the changing of an essentially agricultural society into a richer industrial one, the role of *zuppa* as the daily basic nutritional staple is diminished, and the traditional preparations have been trimmed and adapted to modern requirements of nutrition, taste, and not least, food fashions. But even so, especially in the old versions, no other dish can give as clear an indication of a region's economy, geography, and history. If this is true and valid for every country, it becomes particularly varied and interesting for Italy because its geography—and resulting economy—ranges from the highest mountains in Europe to the seas that surround it on three sides to the many rich and poor islands off its coasts, from some of the most fertile and generous plains to the most arid and ungiving lands. Moreover, Italy's position in the middle of the Mediterranean, at the crossroads of Europe and the Far East, historically has attracted invaders and conquerors from the north and from the south, from the east and from the west. The uninvited visitors took much away, but they also left much of their culture, customs, and tastes. We should remember also that until its political unification as a single nation in 1870, Italy was a mosaic of republics, city-states, principalities, and duchies, each with its own individual turf and culture jealously protected from the others. All of this makes for the richness of regional traits, amply reflected in the various cuisines. From Val d'Aosta in the north to Sicily in the south, each region of Italy has its own particular character determined by history, geography, and the nature of its people. But that is just the beginning: Within the same region, there are many substantial differences between cities, towns, and villages in dialects, mores, and—most important to the hungry traveler—in their gastronomy. *Zuppe* are a leading element in revealing the character of each region.

This book is drawn from our knowledge of the country, of its people and its food. We will introduce the various regions briefly with descriptions derived both from lifelong travels and from our recent meetings with new people.

Our selection of the soups has been made by region but in such a way as to avoid redundancy: Wherever some regions' soups are close variations of others, the most representative will be chosen. But we will point out, also, that sometimes apparently similar recipes, different only in the addition or subtraction of one or two simple ingredients, are quite different in final taste.

Most soup recipes are not, and were never meant to be, chemists' formulas; rather, they are similar to general road maps from which to take reasonable detours, dictated by what your larder holds, by your personal taste and preferences, or by your inspiration of the moment. Adding more of one ingredient or another, or cutting down on the amounts of fats, is permissible, but if the change should do injury to the basic character of a particular soup, then switch to another recipe: There are enough to please your desires.

So, take the best of what the market has to offer, add a pinch of the hearth's warmth and a zest of enthusiasm, stir all into the boiling kettle.

Blow the bugle: Soup's on!

Note: All recipes are given to serve six people. This is because it is practical and just as easy to shop for and prepare a large batch of soup as it is a small one. Most of these soups keep well in the refrigerator and freezer. There is always that unpredictable, rainy and gloomy day when a cup of homemade soup is the most soothing panacea, especially if there is one on hand that you can put on the table with no work and no fuss. The microwave oven was invented for these occasions.

Val d'Aosta

Milk, Rice, and Chestnut Soup
Minestra di latte, riso e castagne

Rice and Turnip Soup
Zuppa di riso alla valdostana

Cabbage, Fontina, and White Bread Soup
Zuppa Valpellinentze

Cheese Soup
Soupe paisanne

Chicken and Almond Soup
Zuppa bianco mangiare

Val d'Aosta

The smooth, four-lane, provincial Route 26 moves north from the elegant and Victorian Turin, leaves behind the Canavese hills, and following the valley carved by the Dora Baltea River, makes its way toward Monte Bianco, the highest peak in Europe. Soon the valley narrows, and the provincial road, the superhighway that leads to France, and the railroad tracks all huddle together, pressing close to the steep walls of the mountains, shying away from the river as from a moody, unreliable wild animal. After prolonged periods of rain or a sudden thaw, it can indeed turn into a murderous beast, trampling away anything in the path of its rage. The Romans, well aware of the river's temper, carved their road high up from its banks, slicing away the mountain granite where it interfered with their path. The Herculean roadwork blazed one of the few gateways across the western Alps. Today's route parallels sections of the old Roman road: The three-inch-deep ruts worn into the stone roadbed by the old cart and carriage wheels attest to the traffic that for centuries moved Roman commerce and might to and from Gallia.

A few miles from its southern border, at Bard, the valley tightens up into a gorge and the road squeezes by, like a thread through a needle's eye, and bends to a more western heading. The panorama changes with the whim of the road. At times the cramped, limited horizon becomes a breathtaking vision of rugged, snow-capped mountains; at others it takes relief in small, sloping pastures as green and just as brilliant as emeralds. You can feel the road climbing with every turn, and finally, fenced in by a crown of white mountains, it levels into a few square miles of flat land. It is here that the Romans, in the first century B.C., built a fortified city and, in honor of Augustus, named it Augusta Praetoria. It grew into today's Aosta, capital and namesake of the valley and of the autonomous region of Val d'Aosta.

Sixty-five miles long by forty miles wide, it is the smallest of Italy's regions, and one of the five untouched by a sea. At the northwesternmost border of the peninsula, Val d'Aosta is like the hyphens between Italy-France-Switzerland: Most of its customs, history, language (French and Italian have equal official usage), and gastronomy reflect its geographical position. Mont Blanc/Monte Bianco is the tallest peak of the Alps, at more than 14,000 feet high, and is surrounded by the St. Bernard, the Gran Paradiso, Monte Cervinio/Matterhorn, and the Monte Rosa. Val d'Aosta nestles among them, an area defined not only by its geography but also by its character.

Val d'Aosta is a winter sports paradise offering some of the best skiing in Europe. The Valdostani boast of the fact that since their side of the Alps faces south, they enjoy sunnier slopes that remain in daylight while the northern sides of the watershed, French or Swiss, are already in chilly shadow.

But you need not be a dedicated skier to appreciate Val d'Aosta's beautiful and rugged nature: Spring, summer, and fall are perfect for mountain hiking and climbing, whitewater rafting and kayaking, gliding and hang gliding, or just sightseeing in the national park of the Gran Paradiso, the protected home and refuge of a long list of mountain flora and fauna.

The stunning and unique beauty of the area is equaled only by its strategic position. Geographically it is one of the few doors in the Alpine wall, a position that politically made it the lock and bolt, the gatekeeper and toll taker of all the traffic between northwest Europe and the Italian peninsula. There is reason to believe that through Val d'Aosta's steep, narrow passes, Hannibal brought his army and its elephants into Italy in 216 B.C., a feat that Napoleon repeated in 1800, leading his army, cavalry, and artillery—50,000 strong—on their way to victory at Marengo. From prehistory on, Val d'Aosta's key points were kept and defended by the strong and powerful of the moment. In the Middle Ages, in a veritable game of king of the mountain, the commanding positions along the valley were kept by seventy-two castles and fortresses, each within watchful sight of the other. Many are in ruins but a number still exist, now beautifully preserved. The passage of different cultures has left Val d'Aosta with a rich cultural and artistic background; at the same time, perhaps as a reaction to strong foreign influences, its people are fiercely independent, consistently loyal to their creeds and beliefs. And above all, because of the harsh nature of the land and its limited space, they are self-reliant: Whatever space the granite of the mountains has left to the soil, it has been carefully nursed and administered.

In the remote mountain hamlets, fields are not measured in acres but in feet; whatever grows tastes more tasty and is treasured more. Here, in terraces as wide as a foothold, grow vineyards at the highest altitude in Europe; in the daytime, the stone pillars that support the trellises store warmth and parcel it back to the grapes during the night. The wines from the grapes are not many or abundant, but they are good. And so are the golden *renette* apples, and the chestnuts and the small *martin sec* pears, and whatever else the soil releases from its clutches. All the local products go to make the region's cuisine, which reflects closely the character of its people. The specialties of the traditional cuisine are not many and none too elaborate, yet in each of the lateral valleys that descend from the high peaks to join the central *vallee* of the Dora Baltea river, there is a twist to the cooking.

A good example is the soup; each valley has a variation on the same theme, relying on the local supplies. Common denominator of all is Fontina, the most prized of the local cheeses. Made immediately after milking, its taste, aroma, consistency, and creaminess will tell a Valdostano in which season and in which valley the cows were pastured. On the list of local foods, beside the ruling *zuppe,* is the *mocetta,* highly flavored, thinly sliced cured meat of mountain goat or chamois; *riso, latte e castagne,* a soup of rice and chestnuts cooked in milk; the sturdy *carbonnade,* a dark stew of beef, onions, and red wine; and *civet alla valdostana,* hare stewed in wine and spiked with fiery grappa. But then there are also some lighter local specialties, such as *costoletta alla valdostana,* a veal cutlet layered with Fontina and prosciutto; or the *tegole d'Aosta,* "Aosta roof tiles," crisp and light almond cookies that are exceptions to the generally stout mountain fare. In the same way, the Valdostani's character is a mix of dedicated seriousness and mountain-like solidity with a love for conviviality and camaraderie. It is a rare occasion when a public place, be it a fashionable restaurant or a humble eatery, does not host a group of Valdostani—young and old—having a glorious time together. Almost de rigueur is a postprandial round-robin of toasts with grappa, the 100-proof grape distillate, accompanied by a chorus of mountain songs.

To be faithful to local folklore, such libations should be had from the *grolla,* the cup of friend-ship: an intricately carved pear-wood vessel with many spouts, which is passed round and round. The contents, sipped directly from the spouts, are a concoction of grappa or *genepy des Alpes* (a liqueur made of local herbs steeped in grappa), hot coffee, and hot red wine. It is a mixture apt to put a smile on your face and melt away any enmity—and the ice on the roof, as well.

It is in the same spirit of camaraderie that a guest at a table is offered first a bowl of soup. The soup tureen is placed in the middle of the table, and its steaming contents, in a convivial gesture similar to breaking bread, are ladled directly into the individual bowls to warm the heart and nourish the body.

The list of purely Val d'Aosta soups is limited: Until 1947 the region has been an integral part of Piemonte, with which it shares many customs. Hence there has been a considerable amount of gastronomic cross-pollination, with many dishes appearing in, and claimed by, both regions.

Milk, Rice, and Chestnut Soup

Minestra di latte, riso e castagne

This soup's signature ingredient is the dried chestnuts. They are available year round in most stores specializing in Italian foods. Their shriveled appearance and hard-as-rock texture disappear once they are soaked overnight, and the soup itself develops a creamy texture once cooked.

6 ounces dried chestnuts

8 cups cold water

1 teaspoon (approximate) salt

1 bay leaf

¾ cup long-grain rice

1½ cups warm milk

1½ tablespoons unsalted butter

Soak the chestnuts overnight in enough water to cover.

Drain the chestnuts, and put them in a soup pot with the cold water, salt, and the bay leaf. Bring the pot to a boil, and then reduce the heat and simmer for about 1 hour, or until the chestnuts are soft to a fork (some may be so soft they have broken up during the cooking). The cooking time may vary according to how long the chestnuts have been dried.

Drain the chestnuts, and reserve the cooking water. Discard the bay leaf and any pieces of inner peel that may be present. Mash about ⅓ of the chestnuts to a paste. Return the mashed and whole chestnuts to the cooking water, bring to a boil, and add the rice. Stir a few times and, after about 10 minutes, add the milk and the butter. Cook for another 4 to 5 minutes, or until the rice is done. Serve immediately.

Note: Cooked chestnuts tend to swell up and absorb liquids. Thus, if the soup is too thick, stir in more warm milk.

Rice and Turnip Soup

Zuppa di riso alla valdostana

Melt the butter in a soup pot. Slice the turnips very thin, add the slices to the pot, and sauté for 5 minutes. Add the rice. Cook and stir another 2 minutes over medium heat, or until the rice begins to crackle. Add the salt and the hot broth and continue cooking for about 14 minutes, stirring occasionally. Add salt to taste. When the rice is cooked, stir in the Parmesan cheese. Allow to rest for 1 to 2 minutes, and serve.

4 tablespoons unsalted butter

2 or 3 turnips (1 pound approximate), washed

1 cup short-grain rice

Salt

8 cups hot chicken broth (or equivalent made with bouillon cubes)

4 tablespoons Parmesan cheese

Cabbage, Fontina, and White Bread Soup

Zuppa Valpellinentze

The Valpelline is one of the valleys that descend from the tip of the Alps to join the central valley, close to Aosta. During a recent trip, we sampled more than a few versions of this soup, each of which was offered as the specialty not only of the establishment but also of its location in the Low, Mid, or High Valley.

This version comes from the high Valpelline valley, where it is exposed to Swiss-German influence.

1 small cabbage, approximately
   1 to 1¼ pounds

3 tablespoons unsalted butter

4 or 5 whole cloves

1 garlic clove

¼ teaspoon freshly grated nutmeg

Salt

Pepper

6 to 12 half-inch slices Italian-
   style white bread, oven-toasted
   (See Basics, page 261)

4 ounces prosciutto, sliced thin
   and cut in strips

5 ounces Fontina cheese, sliced
   thin

1½ quarts well-seasoned beef
   broth, heated

Preheat the oven to 350°F.

Peel off and discard the outer cabbage leaves. Cut out the core, separate the remaining leaves, and boil them in salted water for about 5 minutes, or until limp.

Drain the cabbage leaves, pat them dry with paper toweling, and place them with half the butter in a conveniently sized pan. Peel the garlic and stick the cloves into the garlic clove, and add to the pan. Sauté over moderate heat until the leaves are very tender and well cooked. Mix in the nutmeg. Retrieve and discard the garlic clove. Add salt and pepper as needed, to taste.

Lightly butter an ovenproof soup tureen with a bit of the remaining butter. Make a layer of toast, follow with a layer of cabbage leaves, and top those with a bit of prosciutto and a slice of Fontina. Repeat the layering and finish with the last of the Fontina.

Dot the Fontina with the remaining butter. Add the hot broth just barely to cover and place the tureen in the oven for about 10 minutes, or until the soup has a thin, toasted crust on top. Serve immediately.

Cheese Soup

Soupe paisanne

This winter soup goes also by the name of *zuppa al formaggio.* A real Valdostano would use *Toma,* a partially skim-milk cheese, which is not readily available in the United States. Nice results are achieved with the substitution of Muenster for the *Toma* cheese.

Heat the oven to 350°F.

Line the bottom of an ovenproof casserole with a layer of toast. Add a layer of Fontina, follow with a layer of Muenster and a sprinkle of Parmesan cheese. Make more layers with the remaining ingredients. Pour the hot beef broth over the whole construction.

Place the casserole in the oven for about 10 minutes, or until thoroughly heated.

Note: If you desire a thinner soup, add more hot beef broth.

6 to 12 half-inch slices whole wheat bread, oven-toasted

4 ounces Fontina cheese, sliced thin

4 ounces Muenster cheese, sliced thin

4 tablespoons freshly grated Parmesan cheese

7 cups hot beef broth

Chicken and Almond Soup

Zuppa bianco mangiare

Bianco mangiare is a somewhat archaic way of saying "white diet," which means not only lacking in vivid color but also lacking in spice or rich ingredients. In short: "bland," the kind of food recommended for delicate stomachs, easy to take and to digest.

This soup has been traced back to the fourteenth century's elegant tables, and we conjecture that the presence of almonds, a widely used Middle Eastern ingredient, is a leftover from those periodic incursions of Saracen pirates in the area.

A heightened flavor may be achieved by substituting beef broth for the chicken broth.

4 ounces (approximate) dried-out Italian-style white bread, crust removed

⅔ cup (approximate) milk

3 ounces peeled almonds

½ teaspoon salt

8 ounces skinless, white-meat chicken, boiled

½ teaspoon almond extract (optional)

6 cups chicken broth, heated

Salt

1 cup croutons, oven-toasted

Freshly grated Parmesan cheese

Crumble the dried bread, put it in a bowl, and pour the milk over it. While the bread is soaking, grind the almonds into a powder in a small food processor or by crushing them with a rolling pin. Add the powdered almonds to the milk mixture.

Finely mince the chicken meat and add to the mix. Puree the chicken and milk mixture in a food processor (or pass through a sieve) until you have a smooth paste. Pour it in a soup tureen, and add the almond extract, if using.

Stir in slowly the boiling hot broth. Add salt to taste.

Serve warm, with the croutons and Parmesan cheese on the side.

Piemonte

Onion Soup
Zuppa di cipolle

Vegetable Garden Soup
Minestra giardiniera

Puree of Vegetable Soup
Minestra di verdure passate

Rice and Milk Soup
Minestra riso e latte

Rice and Spinach Soup
Minestra marià

Bean and Rice Soup
Panissa

Egg Pasta and Bean Soup
Tajarin coi fagioli

Chicken Soup
Zuppa di pollo

Meat Ravioli in Broth
Agnolotti in brodo

Piemonte

If we think of a map of Italy as a page of a book, Piemonte—in the upper left corner—would be the very first word of the first paragraph. This propensity for being first conforms not only with its geographical position but also with its prominence in the historical map of Italy. It was Piemonte that sparked the movement leading to Italian unification, and in 1861 the city of Turin, first capital of Italy, under Victor Emmanuel II of Savoy, first king of Italy, flew the *Tricolore,* the first national flag. But then in 1948, when by national referendum the monarchy was abolished, it was Piemonte that supplied the first president of the new Italian Republic. Besides politics, Piemonte boasts a long list of national firsts in many fields, from haute technology to haute fashion to haute cuisine.

These Gallicisms are not an affectation, but are appropriate to the region, which has had a love/hate relationship with France since the time of Gaul, of which it was a province. Known as *Gallia Cisalpina* (This-side-of-the-Alps Gaul) in Caesar's time, on and off throughout history Piemonte was independent from or annexed to France, with the last annexation going from 1798 to 1814. The French influence still manifests itself in the *Piemontesi* dialect, just as much as the Italian influence is alive in the adjacent regions of France.

Turin, ex-capital of Italy, remains the capital of Piemonte and is one of the most elegant Italian cities. Like Paris—and unlike most Italian cities—it was built on a predetermined urban plan and with an eye to its future: The large, tree-lined streets and avenues were planned, in an era of horse and buggy, on such a spectacular scale that they can still accommodate today's traffic. Turin is one of the few old-world cities immune to congenital traffic jams.

Even a casual visitor will realize how the city was doted upon by the long line of dukes and kings of the House of Savoy that presided over its growth. There is something majestic and aristocratic in its architecture, as if its whole core was designed for pomp and circumstance. Most of the streets, squares, and many parks are named after kings, queens, or princes—trunk and shoots of the Savoy tree—and there hardly exists a place in town without a monument to one or another.

You need not be a king to fall for the city: Built on the banks of the majestic Po River and of one of its tributaries, the Dora Riparia, and hedged by rows of green hills, its horizon fenced by the nearby white-crowned Alps, this city has so much to offer that it is surprising how rarely it is considered a traveler's objective. For Turin and the whole region of Piemonte, this anonymity is due in part to the character of its people: industrious, solid, laconic, not easily given to the display of emotions. It is here that industrial Italy was born: Here the car industry took momentum with Fiat and Lancia. The Italian movies, as an industry, began here. Here vermouth was concocted. It was here that cocoa, till then used for beverages, was first made into hard chocolate. Italian radio, and the big band sound, had their birthplace here. And so did Italian fashion as an industry.

Piazza Castello, the heart of the city, must be among the most beautiful squares in the world. Its contour defined by the lace of its porticoes, the Piazza is a truly magical space: It encloses the architectural marvels of the Royal Palace, the Royal Theater, the Church of San Lorenzo, the Prefettura Palace, and as an island in the middle of it all, Palazzo Madama and the Castle, from which the square takes its name.

Turin is, above all, a walkable city, and it is on foot that its graciousness is best savored. From the porticoed embrace of Piazza Carlo Felice (and you can walk a long way under the porticoes in Turin—there are sixteen miles of them!), walk down Via Roma and, sight focused on the elegant shops, cafés, and bookstores along the way, be surprised by the sudden opening of Piazza San Carlo. Here you will understand why the city is often called "Italy's drawing room." The square is huge, yet the pastel colors of the walls, the white stucco flourishes, the decorative wrought-iron street lamps make it a warm environment; people leisurely stroll along or stand in small groups, engaged in conversation, all hushed and comfortable and proper.

Not to be missed is the steep cable-car ride to the Basilica of Superga. Built on top of the highest of the hills surrounding Turin, the Basilica is there to celebrate the victory over the French in 1706, a turning point in the history of Piemonte. As interesting as the architectural and historic values are, it is the view from this dominating position that makes the ascent rewarding. At your feet is the city, and beyond it are the hills, row separated from row by a faint mist. Above these, at the near horizon, rises the sweeping arc of the Alps—on the high peaks of the Moncenisio, of the San Bernard, of the Mont Blanc, of the Gran Paradiso, the perennial snows glisten in a sight that will remain with you forever.

The Alpine valleys are dotted with pastures and dairy farms; the hills of the Langhe and the gentler fields of Alessandria and of the Monferrato are all cloaked in vineyards, vegetable gardens, and fruit orchards. Together with the Vercelli and Novara provinces—huge checkerboards of watery rice fields—they are all a prelude of what, extending toward Venice, will turn into the Pianura Padana, the Po Valley. The Po River, sprung as a rivulet in the Alps at the border with France and fed by a multitude of mountain tributaries, by the time it reaches Turin—in about fifty miles—has become the Mighty Po. It will continue east for another four hundred miles and, crossing the peninsula at its widest point, creates Italy's most fertile region.

Food and wine are taken as seriously in Piemonte as any other aspect of local culture, and with good reason—some of the region's products are unique: Exclusive white truffles from Alba to accompany a fondue of Fontina cheese; *carnaroli, vialone,* or *arborio* rice from Vercelli and Novara, to make a real risotto; a *mocetta* made with Alpine chamois' meat, dried and preserved in Alpine breezes; and a *bagna cauda* made with the crisp, savory vegetables from the Langhe; and the perfect symbiosis of *Stracotto* of *razza Piemontesi* beef cooked in a *Piemontesi* wine. Add the famous *Grissini* (breadsticks) of Turin and its incomparable chocolate-and-filbert mixture *Gianduia,* and you have just scratched the surface of *Piemontesi* culinary wealth.

Some of the best and most prestigious of Italian wines come from Piemonte. The hilly soil sheltered by the Alps, with its misty climate, produces the classy reds of Barbera, Barolo, Barbaresco, Nebiolo, Spanna, Gattinara, and Grignolino and the most noble whites of Gavi and Cortese. Then Asti comes in with Spumante and Moscato and Malvasia and Dolcetto. The list is long, with almost every village and town contributing its own specialty, each very much worth being represented in a connoisseur's cellar.

The *Piemontesi* cuisine is one of sobriety and elegance, of nobility, never overdoing or showing off, letting each aroma and each flavor speak for itself. It is a cuisine at its best in the autumn, when the fragrances of earth and woods are at their highest and the first chills in the air welcome a good glass of red wine and a bowl of soup. . . .

Onion Soup

Zuppa di cipolle

1½ *pounds onions*

6 *tablespoons unsalted butter*

½ *cup dry red wine*

6 *cups beef broth*

Freshly ground white pepper

8 *slices Italian-style bread, oven-toasted*

4 *to 5 ounces Swiss cheese, shredded*

4 *ounces grated Parmesan cheese*

Cut the onions in very thin slivers.

Melt 4 tablespoons of the butter in a large soup pot. Add the onion and cook over a low heat until the onion is tender but not browned. Raise the heat, add the wine, and allow it to evaporate.

Add the beef broth, and bring the mixture to a boil. Cover, lower the heat, and simmer for about 30 minutes.

Preheat the oven to 350°F.

In a large ovenproof soup tureen, make a layer of toast, sprinkle with the Swiss and Parmesan cheeses, and top each with a dollop of the remaining butter. Continue layering until all the bread and cheese have been used.

Pour broth and onions over the layered bread and cheese. Cover the tureen (aluminum foil will do, if you do not have a cover), and place in the warm oven for about 10 minutes.

Vegetable Garden Soup

Minestra giardiniera

The name of this soup suggests the need of a gardenful of vegetables to produce it. In which case, like other vegetable soups or *minestroni* ("big soups"), it is made in a larger quantity than for immediate use. It is common knowledge that the leftover part, reheated and served the next day, is even better than the freshly cooked one so this will serve five, twice. For a no-work elegant variation, see the puree recipe, next page.

Using a large, deep terra-cotta stovetop casserole or heavy soup pot, melt the butter and add the carrots, turnip, potato, celery, leek, peas and sugar. Cook for 3 or 4 minutes, stirring, until the leek and celery are limp. Stir in the vinegar.

Add the thin strips of cabbage to the pot. Add the broth and bring to a boil. When the cabbage is tender, add the lettuce strips. Add salt to taste. Let boil for 5 more minutes, remove from heat, and serve with grated Parmesan cheese.

3 tablespoons unsalted butter

2 medium carrots, peeled and diced

1 medium turnip, peeled and diced

1 medium potato, diced small

1 celery heart, sliced thin

1 leek, white part only, cut in thin rounds

1 cup shelled fresh peas (or frozen)

½ teaspoon sugar

1 tablespoon wine vinegar, or balsamic vinegar

6 ounces (approximate) cabbage (¼ of a small savoy cabbage), cut in thin strips

9 cups beef broth, heated

1 small head Bibb lettuce, cut in thin strips

Salt

Grated Parmesan cheese

Puree of Vegetable Soup

Minestra di verdure passate

Put the cooked soup (preceding recipe) in a food processor or a food mill, and blend until it is a smooth puree.

Add enough warm broth (chicken, beef, or vegetable) to thin the puree into soup consistency. For a very smooth soup pass it through a sieve over a fresh soup pot. Bring to a low boil, and add salt to taste. Stir in 2 teaspoons of butter.

Serve warm with croutons.

Rice and Milk Soup

Minestra riso e latte

Among a long list of quite sturdy soups, every Italian region has one or two extremely simple and delicate ones. They are generally aimed at the very young or the very old but are also recommended for the in-between as a day-after remedy for a too-enthusiastic appreciation of a rich table. In consistency, it should be neither too thick nor too thin: about halfway between a risotto and a pourable soup.

5 tablespoons unsalted butter

1¼ cups arborio rice

6 cups milk, or more as needed

1 teaspoon salt

Dash of nutmeg (optional)

Dash of cinnamon (optional)

Melt the butter in a 3- to 4-quart soup pot. Add the rice and cook, stirring, until the rice begins to crackle. Add the milk and the salt, and bring the pot to a boil. Lower the heat—keeping an eye on the pot, as it can easily boil over—and cook about 15 minutes, stirring occasionally. Stir in the nutmeg and/or cinnamon, if using. When the rice is cooked, check for texture and stir in more warmed milk, if necessary, to obtain the desired consistency. Serve warm.

Rice and Spinach Soup

Minestra marià

Marià, in the *Piemontese* dialect, goes for the Italian *maritata,* or married. Indeed this soup weds two ingredients of which the *Piemontesi* are particularly proud: rice and vegetables, especially spring vegetables, when they are at their most tasteful and tender. In the United States, with this soup in mind, it is worthwhile to seek out a farmer's market that carries fresh spring spinach. Frozen spinach is more than adequate at other seasons.

If using fresh spinach, wash and drain, discarding any coarse stems, and chop the remaining leaves. Melt the butter in the soup pot over a moderate heat, and add the spinach. Add the salt. Stir and cook until spinach is limp. Add the boiling broth.

(If using frozen spinach, add it directly to the boiling broth with the salt and the butter.)

When the mixture returns to a boil, stir in the rice. Bring back to a boil and continue cooking, stirring occasionally, for 15 to 20 minutes, or until the rice is cooked.

Beat the egg and the Parmesan cheese in a soup tureen. When the rice is cooked, pour the rice and spinach soup into the tureen. Stir and serve immediately.

10 ounces fresh spinach leaves (or 1 ten-ounce package frozen, chopped spinach)

6 cups beef broth (or equivalent made with bouillon cubes), heated to boiling

4 tablespoons unsalted butter

½ teaspoon salt

1 cup short-grain, arborio, or vialone rice

1 egg

3 tablespoons grated Parmesan cheese

Note: Depending on type, the rice will absorb more or less broth. Adjust the broth quantity to achieve a soupy, pourable consistency.

Bean and Rice Soup

Panissa

This *panissa* is one version of many substantial one-dish meals traditionally eaten by the *Piemontese* rice farmers. Some versions are claimed by the town of Novara, and others by the town of Vercelli. Nearly all of them use the same locally grown ingredients, give or take an ounce or two of anything. They may vary from a soupy to a spoon-stands-in-it consistency: A point between the two extremes may be obtained by varying the amounts of liquids. Whatever the final consistency, this recipe will feed six rice farmers with very robust appetites.

1 celery rib, minced coarsely

1 carrot, minced coarsely

½ small cabbage (10 to 12 ounces), trimmed and sliced thin

6 plum tomatoes (fresh if possible), peeled and chopped

3 ounces pork rind, cut in 1 × 3–inch strips (optional)

2½ quarts water

Freshly ground pepper

4 ounces lean salt pork

1 to 2 sweet Italian sausages (6 to 8 ounces total), casings removed

1 small onion

4 tablespoons unsalted butter

(Cont.)

In a large soup pot, combine the celery, carrot, cabbage, tomatoes, the pork rind, if using, the water and pepper. Bring the mixture to a boil. Cover, lower the heat, and simmer 10 to 15 minutes, or until the vegetables are tender.

Chop the salt pork, the sausage, and the onion coarsely and place them with the butter in a second soup pot. Add the rice and cook, stirring, over high heat, until the rice starts to crackle. Slowly stir in the red wine.

Add the cooked vegetables and their liquid. Bring to a boil, lower the heat, and simmer until the rice is cooked, about 14 minutes. Stir in the kidney beans and their canning liquid, and heat thoroughly.

Remove the pot from the heat. Add salt to taste. Serve hot or at room temperature (in which case it will be a thicker soup.)

1 cup arborio or short-grain rice

1 cup dry red wine

2 cups canned kidney beans, undrained

2 teaspoons salt

Egg Pasta and Bean Soup

Tajarin coi fagioli

Tajarin is the *Piemontesi* name for *taglierini*, quick-cooking egg pasta noodles, about one-eighth of an inch in width and a delicate contrast to the sturdier beans.

In a soup pot over medium heat, sauté the minced salt pork, onion, celery, garlic, and basil in the olive oil until the onion and celery are limp.

Add the water and bring the pot to a boil. Add the salt, potatoes, and tomatoes. Return to a boil. Cover, lower the heat, and simmer about 20 minutes, or until the potatoes are tender.

Add the kidney beans and their liquid. Bring the soup back to a boil and add the pasta. Cook until the pasta is al dente. Serve hot or at room temperature.

3 ounces lean salt pork, minced

1 onion, minced

1 celery rib, minced

2 cloves garlic, minced

5 basil leaves, minced

2 tablespoons olive oil

6 cups water

1 teaspoon salt

2 potatoes (12 ounces, approximate), peeled and cut in small cubes

3 plum tomatoes (canned or fresh), peeled, seeded, and chopped

(Cont.)

2 cups canned kidney beans,
   undrained

2-egg batch pasta (pages 256–258)
   cut in ⅛-inch-wide noodles,
   or 8 ounces prepared fresh
   fettuccini- or egg noodles

Chicken Soup

Zuppa di pollo

The well-known restorative properties of chicken soup are here reinforced by the egg yolks, considered strength-givers. The yolks also add a pleasant creaminess.

4 egg yolks, at room temperature

4 tablespoons grated Parmesan
   cheese

1 tablespoon lemon zest

½ teaspoon freshly grated nutmeg
   (optional)

½ teaspoon white pepper

1 pound chicken meat, boiled

6 cups chicken broth, heated to
   boiling

6 to 8 ounces Italian-style white
   bread, cubed and oven-toasted,
   or equivalent in commercial
   unflavored croutons

Break the eggs into a soup pot (preferably a stovetop terra-cotta casserole). Add the Parmesan cheese, lemon zest, nutmeg, if using, and white pepper, and beat until smooth.

Cut the chicken into small cubes and mix it lightly with the beaten egg mixture.

Add the boiling broth. Stir and hold over a low heat until the soup has heated thoroughly.

Serve with the oven-toasted cubed bread, or the croutons, if using.

Meat Ravioli in Broth

Agnolotti in brodo

The filling for these soup-bound ravioli (called *agnolotti* in Piemonte) is a medley of beef, pork, sausage, calves' brains, and eggs, all seasoned with nutmeg and Parmesan cheese.

There are any number of different ways of filling ravioli, which are basically the result of planned leftovers saved and set aside for the purpose—a mixture of boiled, baked, or roasted veal, beef, and pork. To remain faithful to the spirit of the various versions, the meats in this recipe are a suggestion, the final mix dictated by those special morsels of cooked meats saved in the freezer, waiting to be turned into *agnolotti*.

If you choose to use the calves' brains: Put the vinegar and about 4 cups of water in a small pot; bring to a boil and then add the calves' brains. Simmer about 5 minutes. Drain the brains from the pot and remove any membranes or gristle.

Boil the chicory for 5 minutes. Drain, squeeze dry, and chop coarsely. Sauté it briefly in a pan with the butter.

Combine the calves' brains, chicory, Italian sausage, beef, and roast pork in the bowl of a food processor and mince finely. Add the egg. When a reasonably smooth paste has been achieved, add the Parmesan, salt, nutmeg, and white pepper. Mix well. The mixture should be easily shaped into half-teaspoon-sized balls. Depending on the moisture of the various ingredients, the final mixture may be too wet or too dry. Adjust by adding more cheese or more broth.

Make the pasta (pages 256–258) and then, using the prepared meat mixture as a filling, the ravioli (page 258).

FOR THE FILLING:

3 tablespoons vinegar (optional)

3 ounces calves' brains (optional)

6 ounces chicory (½ small head, or equivalent of escarole, Swiss chard, or spinach)

3 tablespoons unsalted butter

1 sweet Italian sausage (approximately 3 ounces), casing removed

6 ounces boiled (or roast) beef

3 ounces roast pork (or ham)

1 large egg

4 tablespoons Parmesan cheese, plus more for garnish

½ teaspoon salt

(Cont.)

1 teaspoon freshly grated nutmeg

½ teaspoon white pepper

FOR THE PASTA:

1 two-egg recipe (page 256)

FOR THE BROTH:

6 cups beef broth (page 252)

Cook the ravioli in the boiling broth for about 5 to 10 minutes.

Serve with the broth and with a sprinkle of freshly grated Parmesan cheese.

Lombardia

Minestrone
Minestrone alla milanese

Misshapen-Pasta and Vegetable Soup
Maltaià

Cream of Asparagus Soup
Crema di asparagi alla milanese

Pumpkin Soup
Minestra di zucca

Rice and Parsley Soup
Riso e erbette

Rice and Cabbage Soup
Minestra di riso e verze

Rice and Chicken-Liver Soup
Minestra di riso e fegatini

Rice and Frogs' Legs Soup
Ris e ran

Tripe Soup
Busecca-minestra di trippa

Lombardia

We believe that every place has a perfect season, one at which it is at its best. For us, Lombardy is best in winter. Then, the misty, foggy weather gives a different dimension to the region; it acquires a softer quality. The glaring neon lights of Milan give gentle colored glows to the gray fog; the sounds are muffled. In the mist, the massive, overwhelming stone-and-marble bastions of the Castello Sforzesco and the hundred-pinnacled, one-thousand-statued Duomo appear as fabled places, barely resting on the ground, their outlines softened and fading away, ending nowhere, leaving their completion to your imagination. The wet streets and squares become glistening mirrors, rendering the shivering image of buildings, hurrying people, and traffic as in an impressionist painting.

These Lombard winter attributes are not just in Milan; they apply similarly to the provincial cities, towns, and villages. Tall bell towers pierce the fog like periscopes for the urban cocoons below; in winter, the brown-pink bricks of Po Valley clay take now deeper, now lighter hues. There are no brassy primary colors—it all takes the soft-edged warmth of pastels.

Lombardy is rich, and it is important. It has been so for many centuries, for a number of favorable factors: the geographical position that puts it at the intersection of European communication routes, historical events mastered by a few strong families, the natural richness of the soil, and not least, the eager work ethic of its people. Lombardy is Italy's heartbeat and engine: Most of the commercial and industrial heavyweights—from international finance and banking to textile, chemical, clothing, publishing, printing, advertising, automobile, aviation, heavy and light machinery, and tire and rubber enterprises—can be found in Lombardy. It is at the world's leading edge of industrial design and of all that is stylish and fashionable.

Lombardy is not only vital but also beautiful, chock-full of rich man-made artworks. They complement its natural beauty: Lake Como and Lake Garda, in any season, are deservedly famous international destinations, and so is the Valtellina, the beautiful green space that climbs north from the Po Valley and reaches the Alps at the Swiss border. In winter, the interminably flat fields of the Po Valley, marked only by the rows of the poplars' and elms' vague shadows, seem swollen and pregnant with the promise of the bounty to come. And bounty it is: wheat, corn, soy, potatoes, sugar beets, and the whole gamut of greens and fruits. And then the tastiest of beef and pork, to be transformed into a most inventive list of sausages and salami, and a rich dairy industry that for centuries has fed the rest of Italy with the sweetest of creams and butters. Its cheeses can be found in the fanciest shops of Tokyo, Sydney, or New York: Bel Paese, Gorgonzola, Mascarpone, Grana, Stracchino, Taleggio. . . . Its bounty is what makes the gastronomy of Lombardy so fragmented: A particular dish, stemmed from a local specialty, is totally ignored ten miles down the road where another local product springs up to dominate the table; another five miles and both are forgotten in favor of a third. Perhaps where all these microgastronomies meet is around a brick of sweet butter and a chunk of Grana cheese, without which any Lombard meal seems incomplete. It is through them that the pastures' fragrances of spring, summer, and fall reach the table.

But it is especially in winter that, besides their unmistakable look, Lombard places have an individual aroma: A nostalgic nose will distinguish Brescia from Cremona, Como from Mantua, Bergamo from Varese. It is as if fog and mist entrap the towns' scents and let them linger for you to savor. And they carry food memories: Cremona of candies, sweet *mostarda,* crunchy *torroni;* Mantua of warm, comforting *bollito misto;* Brescia of steaming *minestre* and *minestroni.* If you wish to cuddle your soul in winter, have a meal at a Lombardy table: the gray, misty cold outside and the steamed-up windows inside do not induce gloom but create the right environment for the warm, heartwarming food and ruby-red wine. Lombardy in winter: It spells well-being, contentment.

Minestrone

Minestrone alla milanese

Minestrone, meaning "big soup," is known to the world as much as pizza or pasta, so that many think that Italian soups begin and end with minestrone. This belief is fostered by the fact that almost every Italian region has its own version of the big soup. Among them is that of Milan—and even here every cook seems to posses the "real" recipe, which always includes rice.

It utilizes many and varied vegetables (fresh or canned) according to season and market. For an authentic version, strips of pork rind are essential, but new generations of cooks tend to do without it.

Like many soups, minestrone begins with a mince of basic flavorings and then goes on to the real contents. It may be served warm as soon as made or made ahead of serving time and served at room temperature. It can be refrigeratated for two to three days but must not be frozen, since cooked rice loses its texture when frozen.

Chop coarsely the celery, onion, carrot, salt pork, sage, and basil. Mince them finely by hand or in a food processor.

Add the olive oil to a large soup pot and sauté the mince until limp and golden.

Add the hot water and salt to the pot, raise the heat, and bring to a boil.

While the water is coming to a boil, slice the celery, carrots, and 2 of the potatoes in roughly ½-inch cubes. Break the cauliflower into flowerets. Place the celery, carrots, potatoes, and cauliflower in the water while you prepare the other vegetables.

Slice the third potato with a vegetable peeler into paper-thin slices; chop the zucchini into ½-inch rounds. Cut the

FLAVORINGS:

1 celery rib, with leaves

1 onion, quartered

1 carrot, peeled

2 to 3 ounces lean salt pork

3 to 4 fresh sage leaves, or 1 teaspoon dried sage

6 fresh basil leaves

3 to 4 tablespoons olive oil

FOR THE SOUP:

9 cups water, heated

2 teaspoons salt (approximate)

2 *celery ribs*

2 *carrots, peeled*

3 *potatoes, peeled*

¼ *cauliflower*

2 *medium zucchini*

¼ *head escarole*

¼ *head chicory*

¼ *small cabbage, cored*

1 *cup fresh (or frozen) peas*

4 *plum tomatoes (fresh or canned), peeled and chopped*

1 *cup medium-grain rice (see Rice, page 247)*

1 *cup canned kidney or shell beans, drained and rinsed*

6 *tablespoons grated Parmesan cheese, or as needed*

escarole, chicory, and cabbage into ½-inch strips. Add these, the peas, and the chopped plum tomatoes to the soup pot. Bring to a lively boil, and stir in the rice. Lower the heat, and let simmer for about 14 minutes, or until the vegetables and rice are tender.

Mash half the kidney beans and add them to the soup pot along with the remaining beans. Cook another 5 minutes or as needed, depending on how thick you wish the soup to be. In winter, serve hot, topped with the Parmesan cheese. In the summer, fill the soup plates, let them cool to room temperature, and then serve.

Misshapen-Pasta and Vegetable Soup

Maltaià

Maltaià, in dialect, means something that is poorly or roughly cut, misshapen. In this case, it is the homemade pasta that is cut in uneven shapes. It is the pasta's particular texture that gives an added attraction to the tasty vegetable soup.

With a pastry wheel or sharp knife, cut the rolled-out pasta sheet into strips about ¼ inch wide, and then cut these haphazardly on the diagonal in variable lengths of 2 to 2½ inches, to obtain uneven sized and shaped lozenges. Let pasta rest on a lightly floured surface or on clean kitchen towels.

In a soup pot, sauté the minced salt pork, parsley, garlic, onion, and basil in the olive oil until the mince is lightly browned.

Cut the celery, carrot, and potatoes into small cubes. Peel and chop the tomatoes. Add these four vegetables and the beans to the pot with roughly 2 quarts of water to cover.

Add salt and bring to a boil. Lower the heat, and cook slowly at a simmer for about 45 minutes, or until the vegetables are very tender and the soup has thickened.

Return to a boil, add the pasta, and cook until al dente—cooked but still firm.

Serve warm or at room temperature, with the Parmesan cheese.

FOR THE PASTA:

1 three-egg batch homemade pasta (see pages 256–258), rolled thin as for fettuccine (or 8 ounces commercial fresh fettucine)

FOR THE SOUP:

3 ounces lean salt pork, minced

12 flat-leaf parsley sprigs, minced with stems removed

1 garlic clove, minced

1 small onion, minced

4 to 5 leaves fresh basil, minced

4 tablespoons olive oil

2 ribs celery

1 carrot, peeled

2 medium potatoes, peeled

3 to 4 fresh, ripe plum tomatoes

1 pound fresh kidney beans, shelled (or 2 cups canned)

2 quarts water, or as needed to cover

1 teaspoon salt

Freshly grated Parmesan cheese

Cream of Asparagus Soup

Crema di asparagi alla milanese

3 pounds fresh asparagus, or 2 ten-ounce packages frozen asparagus spears

4 cups milk

3 cups chicken broth

5 tablespoons unsalted butter

2 tablespoons olive oil

½ cup unbleached all-purpose flour

1 teaspoon salt

3 egg yolks

½ cup light cream

4 tablespoons grated Parmesan cheese

6 slices Italian-style white bread, oven-toasted

If using fresh asparagus, break off the inedible part of the stem (it breaks easily where the edible part begins) and discard. Cut the tops in inch-long pieces and place in water to soak. (If using frozen asparagus, defrost.)

Heat the milk in one pot and the broth in another.

In a large 4-quart soup pot, heat 3 tablespoons of the butter and the olive oil. Then, stir in the flour and keep stirring over the heat until well mixed. Cook for another minute to obtain a pale roux. Slowly pour in the hot milk, stirring with a whisk as you pour, and follow with the hot broth.

When the liquids have combined with the roux to become a thin cream*, add the asparagus, and return to a boil. Lower the heat and simmer until the asparagus is tender— about 1 minute for frozen asparagus and about 5 for fresh.

Add salt to taste, and add the remaining butter.

Place the egg yolks and the cream in a warm soup tureen along with 2 tablespoons of the Parmesan cheese. With a whisk, beat together the yolks, cream, and cheese, and then pour the boiling soup slowly into the tureen and stir. Serve hot, accompanied by the toasts.

*Variation: Cook the asparagus in boiling water until very well done, then drain. When sufficiently cool, pass through a strainer to puree. Stir puree into the warming thin cream, cook for 1 to 2 minutes, and proceed.

Pumpkin Soup

Minestra di zucca

The pumpkin evokes visions of fall's brilliant foliage and Halloween goblins, as well as pure American manifestations like pumpkin pie. We tend to think of the round, yellow vegetable as a national exclusivity. Yet of all the varieties of pumpkin, the *Cucurbita pepo*—commonly called the American pumpkin—is the most widely grown in Italy.

If using fresh pumpkin: Peel it, discard the seeds, and chop coarsely. Bring a large pot of salted water to a boil. Add the pumpkin and cook until very tender, about 20 to 30 minutes.

Drain it well and, with a food processor or a food mill, turn it into a puree. Place the puree, or the canned pumpkin, if using, in a large soup pot.

Cut the leeks into very thin slices and sauté in a small pan with 2 tablespoons of the butter and a pinch of salt. When leeks are limp, add them and their pan juice to the pumpkin puree.

Warm the milk almost to the boiling point and pour it slowly, stirring it, over the pumpkin. Stir in the sugar, add more milk if you prefer a thinner soup, and set the heat to keep the pot hot but not boiling.

Break the uncooked pasta into small pieces. In a separate pot, bring about two quarts of lightly salted water to a boil and cook the pasta in it. When cooked, drain the pasta and add to the pumpkin soup. Stir in the remaining butter and the Parmesan cheese. Transfer to a soup tureen and serve topped with a sprinkle of minced parsley.

2½ pounds pumpkin, or 20 ounces canned pumpkin puree

Salt

3 leeks, white part only

4 tablespoons unsalted butter

6 to 8 cups milk

½ teaspoon sugar

6 ounces thin spaghetti or vermicelli

2 to 3 tablespoons grated Parmesan cheese

2 tablespoons chopped fresh parsley

Rice and Parsley Soup

Riso e erbette

This is a most simple, traditional Milanese soup, with the few ingredients bringing the best out of each other. *Best* is the key word: The soup must be made with excellent beef broth, good Italian rice, and the freshest, most fragrant parsley.

8 cups beef broth

1¼ cups medium-grain rice
   (see Rice, page 247)

2 four-ounce bunches flat-leaf
   parsley, minced with stems
   removed

2 teaspoons unsalted butter

Grated Parmesan cheese

Bring the broth to a boil. Add the rice, bring back to a gentle boil, and cook 14 minutes, or until the rice is tender.

Stir in the minced parsley and the butter. Serve in warmed soup plates. Add the Parmesan cheese as desired.

Rice and Cabbage Soup

Minestra di riso e verze

3 ounces lean salt pork, minced

1 garlic clove, minced

1 small onion, minced

6 sprigs flat-leaf parsley, minced
   with stems removed

In the soup pot over medium heat, sauté the minced salt pork, garlic, onion, and parsley in the olive oil and 2 tablespoons of the butter until the mince is lightly browned.

Chop the tomatoes and add to the pot. Stir and cook for 5 minutes. Add the broth and bring it to a boil, then add the thinly sliced cabbage. When the mix returns to a boil, stir in the rice. Lower the heat to medium and cook about 15 minutes, stirring occasionally, until the rice is tender.

Remove from the heat, stir in the remaining 2 tablespoons butter and the Parmesan cheese, and serve.

2 tablespoons olive oil

4 tablespoons unsalted butter

3 or 4 peeled plum tomatoes (fresh or canned)

7 cups beef broth, heated

½ head cabbage (1 pound, approximate), core removed, cut in thin slivers

1 cup medium-grain rice (see page 247)

4 tablespoons grated Parmesan cheese

Rice and Chicken-Liver Soup

Minestra di riso e fegatini

In a large soup pot, bring the broth to a boil and slowly add the rice. Return to a boil, and cover. Lower the heat and simmer about 14 minutes, stirring two or three times.

While simmering, clean the chicken livers and cut into small pieces. Sauté in the butter over medium heat for 2 to 3 minutes, stirring. When lightly browned, add the wine and cook until it has nearly evaporated. Stir in the parsley.

When the rice is almost cooked, add the livers and their pan juice, and the grated Parmesan cheese. Cook until the rice is tender.

Taste for salt and adjust if necessary. Pour the soup into a tureen and serve immediately.

8 cups beef broth

¼ cup short-grain rice (see page 247)

8 ounces chicken livers

2 tablespoons unsalted butter

⅓ cup dry white wine

1 tablespoon minced flat-leaf parsley

4 tablespoons grated Parmesan cheese

Rice and Frogs' Legs Soup

Ris e ran

The northwest corner of Lombardy shares with Piedmont the largest rice paddies in Italy. The watery milieu is particularly suitable to a large population of plump frogs, and in that region rice and frogs frequently appear in gastronomic company.

1½ to 2 pounds (approximate) frogs' legs, fresh or frozen

1 onion

2 celery ribs

4 tablespoons unsalted butter

3 tablespoons olive oil

1 teaspoon salt

¼ teaspoon white pepper

¼ cup dry sherry or dry white wine

7 cups beef broth, heated

1 cup medium-grain rice (see page 247)

2 tablespoons finely minced flat-leaf parsley

Freshly grated Parmesan cheese

Boil the frogs' legs for 5 minutes in approximately 2 quarts of lightly salted water. Scoop out the legs and, when reasonably cool, remove the bones and set the meat aside.

Finely chop the onion and the celery together and place in a large soup pot. Add the butter and oil and sauté over medium-high heat until the onion begins to brown.

Add the frog meat, salt, and white pepper, and sauté, stirring for 2 minutes. Raise the heat, add the sherry, and when almost evaporated, add the hot broth. Bring the mixture to a boil, add the rice, and cover. Lower the heat and cook for 14 minutes at a simmer, stirring several times.

When the rice is tender, stir in the minced parsley and serve immediately with freshly grated Parmesan cheese.

Tripe Soup

Busecca-minestra di trippa

The stomach lining of cattle, tripe is widely accepted and used in all Italian provinces (as well as most European cuisines) but, as with other internal organs, it is not appreciated much in America: a culturally acquired taste, perhaps, or a preconceived idea; yet there are enough connoisseurs around who go for it. Tripe does not have much taste of its own, but it readily acquires soups' or sauces' flavors, to which it adds its own texture.

Cut the prepared tripe in ¾ × 2½-inch strips.

Cut the onion, leek, celery heart, and carrot in thin slices. Peel the potato and cut it in small cubes. Cut the cabbage in thin strips.

In a big soup pot over medium heat, melt 1½ tablespoons of the butter with the salt pork strips. Add the onion and the leek and sauté. When the onion and leek have become slightly golden, add the celery and carrot. Stir well and cook 3 minutes, then add the tomatoes.

Mix well and cook about 10 minutes before adding the tripe and the broth. Bring to a boil, and add the cabbage and the potato.

Bring once more to a boil and cook about 10 minutes, or until the potatoes are done. Add the beans and cook another 5 minutes. (Depending on the consistency of the soup, you may want to add more broth or water.)

During the last cooking of the soup, fry the bread in the remaining 1½ tablespoons of butter and the olive oil, and set aside on paper toweling.

Serve the soup warm, accompanied by the Parmesan cheese and the buttered toast.

1½ pounds veal tripe, cooked (page 249)

1 medium onion

1 leek, white part only

1 celery heart

1 small carrot

1 potato

½ small green cabbage

3 tablespoons unsalted butter

2 slices lean salt pork, cut in very thin strips

1 cup crushed, peeled tomatoes (canned or fresh)

7 to 8 cups chicken broth, heated

1 cup cooked kidney beans

6 slices Italian-style white bread

2 tablespoons olive oil

6 tablespoons grated Parmesan cheese

Trentino–Alto Adige

"Toasted Flour" Soup
Zuppa di farina abbrustolita

Trento Pearl Barley Soup
Orzetto alla Trentina

Mushroom Soup
Minestra di funghi

Egg and Mushroom Soup
Zuppa d'ova e funghi

Rice, Potato, Bean, and Leek Soup
Minestra di riso, patate, fagioli e porri

Omelet Soup
Minestra di frittata

Dumplings in Broth
Canederli in Brodo

Goulash Soup
Minestra di goulash/goulashsuppe

Trentino–Alto Adige

Skirting Lake Garda on our left we follow the Val Lagarina, the valley that leads us north from Verona to Trento, and we enter the Trentino–Alto Adige region. A sea of vineyards flanks the road on both sides, extends throughout the length and breadth of the valley, and rises to the bordering hilltops. The vines are grown in pergola fashion, suspending leaves and grapes in a wavy carpet a few feet above the ground. From the high perspective of the road, the wall-to-wall vineyards have the appearance of gentle green waves.

The valley is daughter to the Adige, one of the great Italian rivers. Born in the Tyrolean Alps, it goes by Bolzano and then Trento, cuts through Verona, and goes on to join the Po in its delta and plunge into the Adriatic barely south of Venice. The Adige's fertile banks have been particularly hospitable to vineyards for more than three thousand years and have since been producing excellent wines. Their appreciation was passed on by the Etruscans to the Romans, then to Venetian merchants and to Austrian landlords, and now, through exported superior Merlots and Chardonnays and fashionable Pinot Grigios, to the rest of the world.

Glorious mountain views, crystal clear on an autumn day, beckon us north. The names of villages, towns, rivers, and mountain peaks make us aware that we are treading on sacred soil. The generations—like mine—that came of age between the two world wars were taught to give to this ground the value and the respect due an altar. This was the heart of World War I, our war. We were brought up to honor in deed and thought all the martyrs and all the heroes and all the places and all the mountains and rivers that were the actors and stage of that conflagration—all the murderous battles, the bloody defeats, and, after four years of trench war and slaughter, finally Vittorio Veneto, the name of our victory. The Alps' watershed line was made to mark the new border, and all foreign lands south of it became Italian. It inspired melancholy or fiery Alpine chants, mournful poems and triumphal songs, and a romantic-heroic literature fanned by Gabriele D'Annunzio and, later, by Hemingway. Our generation sang and recited and read it all, with heads uncovered and hearts overflowing.

Today, Trentino–Alto Adige is an autonomous region formed by the two independent provinces of Trentino, with Trento as its capital city, and Alto Adige/South Tyrol, with Bolzano/Bozen as capital. In this province, the widely used "/" may be interpreted as a unifying or a dividing sign, depending on your point of view. After long-fought, and at times violent, vicissitudes, in 1972 the ethnic Austrian 68 percent majority won the right to its own language, schools, and promulgation of its culture. Alto Adige/South Tyrol now has two official languages, German and Italian. Who loses out are the Ladini, a 4-percent minority, the original inhabitants of the area since before the Etruscans. Every written manifest or sign has its ethnic mirror, separated or united by a slash. But then, given its proximity to the Brenner/Brennero Pass, one of the few Alpine gateways between Italy and Central Europe, a transition "slash" is what this border region has always been, its strategic value appreciated throughout history by invaders and defenders, by popes and emperors.

The incredible number of castle-fortresses and manors (three hundred fifty in Alto Adige alone) add to the natural beauty of the area, which is already exceptional. The many mountain massifs, bejeweled by sparkling permanent snows and glaciers, are mirrored in and multiplied by the hundreds of emerald green or sky blue mountain lakes. Many of the lakes' shores are like archives of the evolutionary steps of man, tracing his comings and goings in this zone for more than ten thousand years. It was here, in the Paleolithic era, that some primordial, upwardly mobile man made his first shelter away from the caves and moved up to stilted huts built on the shores, creating lake-dwelling communities and then, with the manufacturing of metal artifacts, graduating into the Bronze Age.

Trento is a city of one hundred thousand souls, protected on one side by the rushing Adige River and on the others by rocky peaks and high pastures. In the sixteenth century, Pope Paul III convoked the Council of Trent: Besides the philosophical and ecumenical decisions reached, the assemblage of bishops of the Church and high personages of Charles V's court and their wealthy retinues brought great fame and prosperity to the city for the two decades of its duration.

The influences of Italy and of Austria mix subtly in the architecture, people, and gastronomy of Trento. It is a robust cuisine, as required by mountain climate and activities, especially rich in one-dish energy-packing soups. It reflects the roots of the Trentini who, now elegantly urban, are of definite mountain stock, still major contributors to the Alpini Corps, the strong and rugged Italian mountain troops. The cold climate favors foods easily preserved: smoked meats—beef, pork, horse or donkey, turkey or goose—and also hardy cabbage for krauts/*crauti* and abundant, ubiquitous potatoes.

A good overview of Trento can be had from Dosso, the flat-topped hillock just across the Adige River. From its *belvedere* the city appears below as a three-dimensional map, its architectural features like the city's open history book. The view should be a prelude to a stroll through the handsome city. And when in Trento, do as the Trentini do: Make a stop once in a while to admire the houses' frescoed facades; take a rest at one of the many elegant cafés and have a shot of grappa, the fiery brandy said to be an "Alpino mother's milk." It will not make an Alpino out of you, but it will definitely give a new swiftness to your step.

Following the Adige north of Trento, the vineyards give more and more space to the fruit trees and apple orchards for which the region is famous. In spring with the orchards in bloom and the mountain pastures covered by wildflowers, the whole area competes for a spot among the Seven Wonders of the World.

In Bozen/Bolzano, roughly the same size as Trento, the "/" appears to be mostly a formality. By the widely used German-Gothic lettering, Tyrolese architecture, and palpable Austrian atmosphere, a traveler will realize immediately he is in the heart of South Tyrol. The citizenry is exceptionally and consistently hospitable, yet in a more composed and formal way than the more exuberant and volatile denizens of the regions to the south.

Peter Giovannelli, the manager of the Hotel Grifone and its restaurant, the Belle Epoque, says, "Our province is not big, and most of it is mountains: We have to take good care of what little we have. Quantity for us comes way behind quality." The local cuisine, with its Knödels, Specks, Krauts, Wienerschnitzels, Apfelstrudels, rich Viennese pastries and creams, remains faithful to Austrian roots but also doesn't disdain using traditional Trentino dishes.

The roads winding through Trentino–Alto Adige are smooth and well kept, an invitation to travel, and they deliver at any frequent turn and at any season overwhelming mountain scenery. The admirable cleanliness and tidiness of the landscape could appear staged: white-splotched brown cows choreographed in scrubbed-green pastures; wooden chalets and whitewashed villages positioned just so, to counterbalance the majestic presence of the mountains; waterfalls springing from on high add feathery motion to static scenery, torrents rumbling and foaming down below. . . . It all looks like a poster-perfect picture.

Beside the many urban and natural attractions, a strong magnet to the region are the Dolomites. The jagged, pinnacled mountains, sprouting straight up from velvety pastures, are a treasure that Trentino–Alto Adige has to share with bordering Veneto. If you are heading west from Bolzano, stop at the top of the winding road at the Sella Pass or, farther on, at the Pordoi Pass at sunrise or at sunset. It is as if the mountains' vertical walls of pure Dolomite stone—compacted out of primordial algae and coral reefs—drink in the sun and take its color, the eternal glaciers flashing its passage.

The sweeping view back toward the west reveals what should have been clear from the beginning: The mountains are the hyphen that unites Trentino–Alto Adige and its people. Perhaps the yodeling is different, but their lives, their work, their wine, and their food are the same. You will soon find out that the mountain flower *Stella alpina* is an edelweiss, just as a perfumed glass of Traminer Aromatico is a glass of Gewurztraminer and one of Pinot Bianco is one of Weissburgunder; and then that a *Terlanersuppe* is none other than *Zuppa al Terlano,* and *Knödelsuppe* is *Canederli in brodo.* Different is the sound, but the taste is the same—definite and invigorating.

"Toasted Flour" Soup

Zuppa di farina abbrustolita

This soup, which hails from Bolzano/Bozen, also appears in several versions. Some are more elaborate than others, but the base is the same: "toasted flour," a thinned-down roux. This version is enriched by potatoes, spiked before serving by a splash of red wine vinegar.

Place the potato slices in a soup pot, and add the milk, water, bay leaf, and salt. Bring to a boil, and cover, lower the heat and simmer until the potatoes are tender, about 10 minutes. Retrieve and discard the bay leaf.

In a soup pot over medium heat, sauté the salt pork in the butter. When the pork has rendered most of its fat but is not crisp, slowly stir in the flour, and cook, stirring to avoid lumps, until an amber-colored roux is obtained. Then add the cooked potatoes (breaking up and mashing some in the process) and their liquid. Mix well and cook until very hot. The soup should have a creamy consistency: Adjust by adding hot water if too thick or by boiling it down if too thin. Adjust for salt, if necessary. Stir in the red wine or the red wine vinegar, and serve hot.

1½ pounds potatoes, peeled and sliced thin

3 cups milk

4 cups water

1 bay leaf

1 teaspoon salt

3 tablespoons unsalted butter

6 ounces lean salt pork, minced

1 cup unbleached all-purpose flour

Salt

Pepper

½ cup dry red wine, or 3 tablespoons red wine vinegar

Trento Pearl Barley Soup

Orzetto alla Trentina

There is a full family of *minestre d'orzo* (pearl barley soups) in the Trentino–Alto Adige, where barley takes the place of the rice of the regions more to the south. Main and fixed members of the family are barley and pork products, with a small or large variety of vegetables appearing in secondary roles. *Orzetto* (an endearing diminutive of *orzo*) is a good representative for the whole family.

1 small onion, minced

2 to 3 sage leaves, minced

2 to 3 basil leaves, minced

4 to 5 parsley sprigs, minced with stems removed

2 tablespoons olive oil

2 tablespoons unsalted butter

4 ounces smoked slab bacon, cut in ½-inch cubes

2 quarts water

1 teaspoon salt

1 ham bone (with some meat on it, if possible)

1 cup pearl barley, soaked in water overnight

1 leek, white part only, sliced thin

1 carrot, cut in ¼-inch cubes

(Cont.)

In a soup pot over medium heat, sauté the minced onion, sage, basil, and parsley in 1 tablespoon of the olive oil and 1 tablespoon of the butter. When the mince is golden, add the bacon and cook until slightly softened. Add about two quarts of water, the salt, and the ham bone, and bring to a boil. Drain the pearl barley, stir it into the pot, and cover. Reduce the heat and simmer for 30 minutes. Then add the leek, carrot, potato, and celery, and cook for another 20 to 30 minutes, or until the barley is swollen and very soft. During cooking, the barley absorbs a great quantity of water. Check from time to time and add more warm water as needed. The final consistency should be a thick but spoonable soup.

Remove the ham bone, stir into the soup the remaining 1 tablespoon oil and 1 tablespoon butter, and the Parmesan cheese. Serve hot with a sprinkle of chives.

Note: To obtain a less creamy soup, some of the barley's starch can be eliminated by rinsing it before cooking.

1 small potato, cut in ¼-inch cubes

1 white celery rib, cut in ¼-inch cubes

4 tablespoons grated Parmesan cheese

2 tablespoons chives, minced (optional)

Mushroom Soup

Minestra di funghi

The moist, old woods of this region, in spring and especially fall, supply a generous harvest of wild mushrooms. Most prized among them are the porcini, with their penetrating, woodsy aroma and delicate nutty taste—qualities that seem to disappear in the few fresh, very expensive ones that make it to this country. Fortunately, aroma and taste are preserved, even somewhat exalted, when the porcini are dried: A few go a long way, sometimes tending to overpower other tastes. In this soup, store-bought white mushrooms are used together with dry porcini to mutual benefit, and they make a most satisfying, delicate soup.

Soak the dry porcini for 15 to 20 minutes in 1½ cups warm water. Clean and cut the fresh mushrooms in thin slices.

Drain the reconstituted porcini, and reserve the soaking water. Clean them of any sand, and chop coarsely. Filter the reserved water into another container through a sieve lined with cheesecloth, or decant it slowly, preventing the sediments from pouring out.

1½ ounces dried porcini mushrooms

10 ounces fresh white mushrooms

1 teaspoon salt

3 tablespoons olive oil

4 tablespoons unsalted butter

½ cup flour

1 cup warm milk

6 cups beef broth (approximate), warmed

2 tablespoons minced flat-leaf parsley

Freshly ground white pepper

In a large pan over medium heat, sauté the white mushrooms, porcini, and salt in the olive oil, stirring frequently, until the mushrooms are cooked and have released some of their moisture. Stir in the reserved water, let it reduce a little, and turn off the heat.

Melt the butter in a soup pot over moderate heat. Add the flour, and stir vigorously with a small whisk. When a smooth paste is reached, add the milk. Cook, whisking, for about 2 minutes.

Stir the sautéed mushrooms and their liquids into the soup pot.

Add all the broth (or a little less for a thicker soup) slowly, stirring. Bring to a boil, and then lower the heat and simmer for 10 minutes.

Serve hot with a sprinkle of minced parsley and freshly ground white pepper to taste.

Egg and Mushroom Soup

Zuppa d'ova e funghi

This soup is called also *minestra montanara*—mountaineers' soup—perhaps because hunting mushrooms is a classic mountaineer's hobby or because, together with the lightness of the mushrooms, the soup also offers energy-giving eggs. The wild mountain mushrooms should be cut in spoon-size pieces to give the soup a chunky texture. On the American market, portabella mushrooms are big and sturdy enough to allow this treatment.

In a soup pot over medium heat, sauté the minced onion and garlic and the salt in the olive oil and butter until the onion is limp. Discard the garlic clove. Mash the bouillon cube, add it to the pot, and stir until it is dissolved. Add the mushrooms. Increase the heat and sauté, stirring, until the mushrooms release their moisture and are lightly colored. Add the warm water, and stir in the parsley. Bring to a boil, simmer for 5 minutes, and remove from heat.

In a soup tureen place the egg yolks, the Parmesan cheese and the milk or cream, and beat thoroughly. Stir in the hot mushroom soup.

Serve immediately with toasted slices of Italian bread.

1 onion, chopped coarsely

1 garlic clove

1 teaspoon salt

3 tablespoons olive oil

2 tablespoons unsalted butter

1 beef bouillon cube

10 ounces portabella mushrooms, cut in 1-inch chunks

7 cups warm water

3 tablespoons minced flat-leaf parsley

4 egg yolks

4 tablespoons grated Parmesan cheese

¼ cup milk or cream

6 slices Italian-style white bread, oven-toasted

Rice, Potato, Bean, and Leek Soup

Minestra di riso, patate, fagioli e porri

7 cups beef broth (or equivalent made with bouillon cubes)

1½ pounds (3 medium-size) potatoes, peeled, cubed

1½ pounds leeks, white part only

½ onion, cut in thin slivers

1 tablespoon olive oil

1 tablespoon unsalted butter

¼ cup dry white wine

¼ teaspoon cinnamon

¼ teaspoon white pepper

1 cup kidney beans, cooked

¾ cup medium-grain rice

Salt

Freshly grated Parmesan cheese

In a soup pot, combine the broth and the potatoes, and bring to a boil. Cut the leeks into thin slices and add to the cooking potatoes. Cover the pot and simmer until well done.

In a small pan over medium/low heat, sauté the onion in the oil and butter. When limp and golden brown, stir into it the wine, the cinnamon, and the pepper. Let it reduce a little, then pour the onion, its pan juices, and the beans into the simmering potatoes. Bring the pot to a boil and stir in the rice. Add salt to taste and cook for about 14 minutes, or until the rice is tender. By the end of cooking, the potatoes and rice may have absorbed most of the broth, turning all into a reasonably thick soup. If too thick, add more warmed broth or water. Serve hot with freshly grated Parmesan cheese.

Omelet Soup

Minestra di frittata

The name is quite a misnomer: The *frittata* (omelet) of the title is more like a crepe, or even a pancake, since the eggs are strengthened by a good amount of flour and milk. But whatever its name, the soup is an elegant and light departure from the otherwise sturdy mountain fare of Trentino–Alto Adige.

Make a smooth batter with eggs, flour, and milk. Stir into it the salt and the minced parsley.

To make the crepes, butter a small omelet pan or frying pan. Add a few tablespoons of the batter, and tilt the pan so that the bottom is barely covered. As one crepe is cooked, put it aside to cool, and continue until all the batter is used.

Roll up each crepe, and cut the rolls in ¼-inch slices. Fluff the slices into strips and distribute them evenly into six soup dishes. Pour the hot broth over them and sprinkle with the chives.

Serve immediately.

3 eggs

*¾ cup unbleached all-purpose
   flour*

1 cup milk

½ teaspoon salt

12 sprigs flat-leaf parsley, minced

*2 tablespoons unsalted butter
   (approximate)*

*7 cups chicken or beef broth,
   heated to boiling*

12 chives, minced

Dumplings in Broth

Canederli in brodo

Canederli is the Italian equivalent of the Austrian *Knödel*. About the closest we can come to describe *canederli* is "superdumplings." They may vary in size a bit, but generally they are slightly smaller than—or as big as—tennis balls. Everything is fair game to make *canederli*—spinach, mushrooms, sausages, liver, spleen, duck, pork, beef—yet the basic ingredient that gives it body is old bread soaked in milk. Once poached, the big dumplings may be served with a sauce, but more frequently they are served in boiling hot broth. The following *canederli* hail from Trento.

1½ pounds Italian-style white bread, dried and cut in 1-inch cubes

2½ cups lukewarm milk

4 ounces smoked bacon

4 ounces salami

2 tablespoons olive oil

3 tablespoons sifted flour, plus more as needed

3 tablespoons minced flat-leaf parsley

2 tablespoons grated Parmesan cheese, plus more as needed for garnish

¼ teaspoon nutmeg

3 eggs

Salt

7 cups beef or beef-and-chicken broth (pages 252 and 253)

Place the bread cubes and the milk in a bowl, and let rest for at least 1 hour.

Cut the bacon and the salami in thin strips, and sauté them with the oil in a small saucepan over moderate heat until lightly golden. Drain well on paper toweling.

Remove the soaked bread from the milk, squeeze it a little to drain excess milk (the bread should be well moistened, not dripping wet). Place the bread in a large bowl and add the sautéed bacon and salami, flour, parsley, Parmesan cheese, and nutmeg. Add the eggs and the salt, and mix well until a compact compound has been achieved, hard enough to retain its shape when rolled into balls. If too soft, add a bit more flour; if too hard, add milk.

With your hands, roll the mixture into balls about 2 to 2½ inches in diameter. Let the *canederli* rest a few minutes.

In a soup pot, bring the broth to a low boil. With a slotted spoon, lower a few *canederli* at a time into the broth and boil them about 5 minutes, or until they float to the surface. Scoop them out into soup dishes, ladle the boiling hot broth over them, and serve at once with additional grated Parmesan cheese.

Goulash Soup

Minestra di goulash/goulashsuppe

This soup is proof, if it were needed, of the Austrian influence on the cooking of Alto Adige. The classic goulash stew is thinned into a soup and, in a show of ethnic integration and mutual benefit, is served with hot Italian bread or polenta.

Mince together the onion, garlic, and salt pork, and sauté them in the olive oil until lightly golden.

Add the beef, cumin, marjoram, and paprika. For a spicier goulash, add the Tabasco sauce. Salt to taste, and add the bay leaf and lemon rind.

When the mixture is well browned, add the broth. Dilute the tomato paste in 1 cup water and add to the broth. Simmer for 45 minutes.

Add the cubed potatoes and continue cooking until the potatoes are very tender; remove the bay leaf and, with a fork, mash some of the potatoes to give the soup a creamy consistency. If too much liquid has cooked away, add more warm broth or water to obtain the right consistency.

Serve hot, accompanied by hot Italian bread or polenta.

1 medium onion

1 garlic clove

3 ounces salt pork

2 tablespoons olive oil

1 pound beef (sirloin or top round), cut in bite-size cubes

¼ teaspoon ground cumin

¼ teaspoon marjoram

½ teaspoon paprika

½ teaspoon Tabasco (optional)

Salt

1 bay leaf

Rind of half a lemon, grated

7 cups beef broth, or lightly salted water

3 rounded tablespoons tomato paste

1 cup water

3 potatoes, peeled and cubed

Veneto e le Tre Venezie

Dainty Venetian Broth
Brodo veneziano in tazza

Venetian Rice and Pea Soup
Risi e bisi

Capuchins' Rice Soup
Minestra di riso alla cappuccina

Lemony Rice Soup
Minestra di riso alla friulana

Celeriac Soup
Zuppa di sedano-rapa

Cream of Mushroom Soup
Crema di funghi

Spinach and Cornmeal Soup
Paparot

Lentil Soup
Zuppa di lenticchie

Bean and Potato Soup
Minestra de fasoi

Bean and Cabbage Soup
Minestra di borlotti e cavolo

Rice and Bean Soup
Ris e fasui

Veneto e le Tre Venezie

~ ❧ ~

Veneto and Venezia Giulia are the two regions of what, together with Venezia Tridentina, once went by the name of Le Tre Venezie—The Three Venices. Sociopolitical shifts have split and recombined the Tridentina into Trentino–Alto Adige and the Giulia into Friuli–Venezia Giulia. Nonetheless, with all the shuffling, Veneto, with Venice as its capital, has remained the root of the whole region.

Venice needs no introduction. Venice's unmistakable calling card *is* Venice, always as new as today and as old as its first people who, seeking refuge from marauding barbarians, took over the one-hundred-odd islets of the lagoon. How it slowly emerged from the sea as a city—how it became a world power against which all other powers had to compare and compete—is a miracle of nature and of history.

Venice has no style; it *is* style. It *has* no art because it is art itself. More than art, it is an artifice, an intrigue of canals as astute as a labyrinth; a gathering of marbles and stones, of statues and columns, of arches and windows as implausible as perfection. It is, in a way, like snow and its flakes, seemingly always the same and yet continually different: Of its hundreds of canal-spanning bridges, not one is like another. Its juxtaposing of architectural styles, of colors and textures, of water and sky, of things that, in any other place, would be formless and offensive, here becomes elegant and radiant.

The brilliance of Venice has frequently blinded the foreigner to the existence of many of her neighboring cities and towns or, at best, made them shine with reflected light, like planets around a sun.

As a physical reminder of Venice, there is hardly a town in the Tre Venezie that doesn't show, in a predominant position, the Venetian winged Lion of St. Mark, its book of Law firmly in its paws. No other symbol embodies such majestic confidence. Like a benevolent sovereign, it seems to say, "I know the way. Obey, and I will lead and protect you . . ." The *or* is unspoken, a mute but strong incentive to behave.

Its gaze is felt wherever one goes in the Tre Venezie, and there is a lot to go to. The whole area is a high-intensity cultural and natural trove. The difficulty is in making a choice of where to go. How do you pass up historied Treviso or colorful Chioggia? Or, just south of the lagoon, the stark, somber Comacchio marshes, born of the Po River delta. And the long line of Ville Venete, the country cottages of the Venetian aristocracy, signed by Palladio and frescoed by Tiepolo and Giorgione and Titian. Giotto's frescoes of the Scrovegni Chapel in Padua, the seventeenth-century masterpieces in the church of the Beata Vergine del Soccorso in Rovigo, the ancient and modern works of the goldsmiths of Vicenza, the Piazza della Libertà of Udine, the Miramare Castle and San Giusto in Trieste. . . . Or the early works of Titian, in his hometown of Pieve di Cadore, at the doorway of the Dolomite Mountains.

Verona, thanks to a foreigner's *Romeo and Juliet,* shines with a unique light of her own. But of all cities, this city is the least appropriate stage for tragedy: Mourning does not become her. Rain or shine, it would be impossible to find a more charming and cheerful place. Its people are smiling and friendly; it is a happy city which could have been invented by a romantic set-designer. The open space of its Roman Arena—second in size only to Rome's Colosseum; the umbrella-shaded, bustling, open-air market of Piazza delle Erbe; the vast yet hushed and intimate Piazza dei Signori; the filigreed Scaligeri's Tombs; the Giusti gardens; the old bridges over the rushing Adige River; the brick-brown city streets and alleys: All are an invitation to walk the boards of that stage. Do so and you will join a cast of thousands: At any hour of the day—and most of a summer night—the whole city is a continuous round-and-round promenade of chatting people. De rigueur is a stop at one of the many pubs for an *ombra,* a "shadow"—a civilized glass of wine and a chat.

All around the city and west to Lake Garda are vineyards: Valpolicella, Bardolino, Amarone, Soave, Prosecco. They all have their place in the roster of classic Italian wines, and they are in good company: Not much farther north, the Friuli vineyards supply some of the best Italian white wines, and all complement the Veneto and Tre Venezie's regional gastronomies. The sophisticated cuisine of Venice, flavored with the spices of which the city was the main trader since the thirteenth century, is only a small chapter. The subtle rice dishes, halfway points between soups and risottos, velvety with young vegetables and delicate fish, soon make room for a larger and sturdier cuisine. Polenta, cornmeal mush, is Friuli's mainstay: Spread on a communal board, it is its own plate and meal at the same time, carrier of sauces and stews. Beans, cabbage, potatoes, and pork are the basic ingredients of a humble larder—and one not so humble, when raw ham becomes the choice prosciutto of San Daniele, Venezia Giulia's small mountain town.

Soups dominate the table—simple, direct, and satisfying, with rice and beans taking the lion's share. The dishes are robust and savory, taking advantage of all that is edible, as a poor peasant cuisine makes obligatory. Of a butchering session, little goes wasted: The "lesser cuts"—liver, heart, kidney, tripe, lungs, udder, blood—will be turned into local gourmet dishes. For centuries, Venetian chefs have held a reputation for creativity and taste. They are the very same who have given us *Risi e bisi, Pasta e fasioi, Polenta e baccalà, Carpaccio, Granzeola, Tiramisù, Pandoro,* and hundred and one different ways of using their radicchio—the maroon round one from Chioggia, or the crimson, feathery one from Treviso. . . .

Dainty Venetian Broth

Brodo veneziano in tazza

In general, Venetian soups are quite sturdy, as becomes a northern climate. This *brodo* is a lighter, "dainty" way to open an elegant meal.

6 slices Italian-style white bread

5 egg yolks

2 tablespoons lemon juice

½ teaspoon salt

¼ teaspoon freshly ground pepper

5 cups beef broth, chilled

Trim the crusts from the bread and cut the bread into ½-inch cubes. Oven-toast until golden.

Place the egg yolks in a 3- or 4-quart casserole, and add the lemon juice, salt, and pepper. Beat with a whisk until smooth, and add 1⅔ cups of the cold broth.

Place the casserole over medium heat and continue to whisk as you add the remaining cold broth. Slowly bring to a boil, then remove from the heat.

Divide the bread cubes into the soup cups and pour the egg broth over the cubes. Serve immediately.

Venetian Rice and Pea Soup

Risi e bisi

The Italian *Riso e piselli*—rice and peas—becomes *Risi e bisi* in the Venetian dialect. It is a revered soup, said to date back to the era of the Doges, when Venice was Queen of the Seas. It is a substantial dish: The Venetians like it almost as thick as a risotto, which is eaten with a fork. However, if you wish a thinner soup, add a cup or two of hot broth at the end of cooking.

Cut the prosciutto in small squares.

Heat the oil and butter in a heavy pot over medium heat. Add the prosciutto, onion, and parsley, and sauté until the onion is limp.

Add the peas and enough water to cover them by about ½ inch, and cook for about 5 minutes.

Add the rice and the broth, and bring to a boil. Reduce the heat and simmer for 14 minutes, stirring frequently, or until the rice is tender.

Serve with a sprinkling of Parmesan cheese.

3 ounces prosciutto

2 tablespoons olive oil

3 tablespoons unsalted butter

1 small onion, minced

2 tablespoons minced fresh flat-leaf parsley

10 ounces fresh shelled peas (or frozen baby peas)

1 cup short-grain rice or Italian arborio

5 to 6 cups chicken broth

Grated Parmesan cheese

Capuchins' Rice Soup

Minestra di riso alla cappuccina

Perhaps it is the monastic austerity of this soup that has earned it its name. Or, perhaps, it is because the Capuchin friars are devoted not only to simplicity but also to good taste.

2 tablespoons olive oil

2 tablespoons unsalted butter

1 small onion, minced fine

5 to 6 flat anchovy filets, mashed to a paste

1 cup short- or medium-grain rice

7 cups beef broth

Salt

2 tablespoons minced fresh parsley

Freshly ground pepper

Combine the oil, butter, and minced onion in a soup pot over medium heat. As soon as the onion begins to color, add the mashed anchovies and the rice. Stir until the rice is well coated and begins to crackle, then add about 1½ cups of the broth, stirring. When the broth has been absorbed, add the remaining broth, cover, and cook for 13 to 15 minutes at a simmer, stirring occasionally. When the rice is tender, the soup should be reasonably thick. If you wish, add a bit more broth for a more liquid consistency. Add salt to taste. Stir in the minced parsley and serve immediately, with freshly ground pepper to taste.

Lemony Rice Soup

Minestra di riso alla friulana

This soup is halfway between a *minestra* and a risotto, which means neither too soupy nor too thick. As Venetians describe it, it should be *all'onda,* which means, if tilted, the dish should be fluid enough to "make a wave" but not spill. What makes it truly different from the usual rice dish is the use of lemon and eggs as its defining elements.

Put the broth and the butter in a soup pot and bring to boil. Stir in the rice, and cover. Lower the heat and cook, stirring occasionally, for about 14 minutes, or until the rice is tender.

In the meantime, beat the egg yolks well in a bowl, and add the lemon juice, beating as you pour.

When the rice is cooked, remove from heat. Slowly stir the egg mixture into the rice. When well mixed, stir in the Parmesan cheese. Serve immediately, with a sprinkle of minced parsley and more freshly grated Parmesan cheese, if desired.

8 cups beef broth

2 tablespoons unsalted butter

1¼ cups short-grain rice

4 egg yolks

Juice of 1½ lemons

3 tablespoons grated Parmesan cheese, plus more as needed for garnish

2 tablespoons minced flat-leaf parsley

Celeriac Soup

Zuppa di sedano-rapa

1½ pounds celeriac (celery root)

5 tablespoons unsalted butter

6 cups beef broth

3 small potatoes (1 pound, approximate), peeled and cubed

Salt

1 cup warm milk (optional)

1 small carrot, finely shredded or grated

Unflavored croutons

Clean, peel, and julienne the celeriac, then blanch it in boiling water for 2 minutes and drain well. Melt 2½ tablespoons of the butter in a soup pot, add the celeriac, and sauté it for 1 minute, stirring until well coated with the butter. Add the broth, bring to a boil, and add the potatoes. Salt to taste. Cover and cook over moderate heat until the potatoes are tender.

For a smooth soup, pass the broth and vegetables through a sieve or food mill into a new pot; place over heat and bring to a boil. Stir in the remaining 2½ tablespoons butter.

If the soup is too thick, add a bit of warm milk to achieve the desired consistency. Serve with a sprinkle of shredded carrot and croutons, if desired.

Cream of Mushroom Soup

Crema di funghi

Soak the dried mushrooms for 15 to 20 minutes in 1 cup of warm water. Clean and slice the white mushrooms and add them to a soup pot with 4 tablespoons of the butter, salt, and garlic, and sauté for 5 minutes. Drain the softened porcini, reserving the liquid. Check the mushrooms for sand, and gently squeeze them dry. Chop coarsely and add to the sautéing white mushrooms. Carefully strain the soaking water through a cheesecloth-lined sieve, and add the liquid to the pot.

Add the parsley, pepper, nutmeg, and Marsala wine and cook another 5 to 8 minutes. Remove from heat.

Make a thin white sauce by melting the remaining 4 tablespoons of butter in a saucepan and adding the flour. Cook, stirring constantly. When well blended, stir in the warm milk. Continue to cook, stirring continuously, over medium heat for at least 4 minutes, or until smooth and thickened.

Add the white sauce to the mushrooms in the soup pot.

Add 1½ cups of the vegetable broth to the soup pot.

Stir and cook over medium heat until hot but not boiling. Add salt to taste. If you prefer a thinner soup, add a bit more broth. Serve immediately.

1 ounce dried porcini mushrooms

1 pound white mushrooms

8 tablespoons unsalted butter

1 teaspoon salt

1 garlic clove, chopped fine

1 cup freshly chopped flat-leaf parsley

Freshly ground pepper

½ teaspoon freshly grated nutmeg

½ cup dry Marsala wine

½ cup unbleached all-purpose flour

4 cups warm milk

1½ to 2 cups vegetable broth (page 254), or 2 vegetable bouillon cubes dissolved in 2 cups water

Spinach and Cornmeal Soup

Paparot

This is a spinach soup enriched by cornmeal (polenta), which gives it the yellow overtones, almost—with the help of some imagination—like those of a little duckling (*paparot* in the dialect of Friuli).

2 pounds fresh spinach

2 garlic cloves

2½ tablespoons unsalted butter

1 tablespoon olive oil

9 cups chicken or beef broth

1 cup fine cornmeal

½ cup all-purpose white flour

Salt

Freshly ground pepper

Wash the spinach carefully, removing the coarsest stems. Cook in the water that clings to the leaves, in a covered pot about 6 minutes (after the water begins to steam). When the spinach is cooked, place it in a colander and squeeze it against the sides to eliminate as much water as possible, and then chop it finely.

Put the garlic, butter, and olive oil in a soup pot and cook over medium heat until the garlic is golden brown.

Remove the garlic cloves, add the spinach, and sauté it for one minute. Add 8 cups of the broth to the pot, bring to a boil, and simmer over a low heat.

Combine the cornmeal and white flour in a bowl. Stirring, add the remaining cup of cold broth slowly, to avoid lumps, and mix well to make a thin batter. Pour the batter slowly into the broth as it simmers, stirring constantly, and let the pot boil for about 15 to 20 minutes, stirring as it cooks. Adjust the thickness of the soup to your taste by adding a little more broth (or warm water) for a thinner soup, or cooking a little longer for a thicker consistency.

Add salt and pepper to taste, and serve.

Lentil Soup

Zuppa di lenticchie

What makes this soup somewhat different from the lentil soups of other regions is the use of anchovies and wine among the flavorings.

Put the lentils in a soup pot with the water and salt. Bring to a boil, then lower the heat to a simmer and cook for 20 to 25 minutes, or until cooked but not overdone. Drain, but reserve the cooking water.

Mince together the garlic, sage, parsley, onion, celery, and anchovies.

In a soup pot, sauté the minced flavorings in the olive oil and cook, stirring, until lightly golden. Add the wine, and stir until almost evaporated. Add the crushed tomatoes and cook for 2 to 3 minutes.

Add the lentils to the pot, and add enough of the reserved cooking water to reach the desired consistency.

Place a slice of the toasted bread in each soup plate, add the soup, and serve immediately.

1 cup lentils

8 cups water

1 teaspoon salt

1 garlic clove

2 sage leaves

5 to 6 sprigs flat-leaf parsley

1 small onion

1 celery rib

6 flat anchovy filets

3 tablespoons olive oil

⅓ cup dry white wine

4 plum tomatoes (canned or fresh), peeled and crushed, or 8 ounces tomato sauce

6 slices of Italian-style white bread, oven-toasted

Bean and Potato Soup

Minestra de fasoi

6 ounces dried kidney beans

8 cups water

1 carrot

2 potatoes, peeled

1 bay leaf

1 teaspoon salt

2 ounces lean salt pork

1 medium onion

1 garlic clove

2 sage leaves

5 to 6 sprigs flat-leaf parsley

1 celery rib

3 tablespoons olive oil, plus more as needed for garnish

Soak the dried kidney beans overnight in enough water to cover; drain. Place the reconstituted beans in a large soup pot with 8 cups of water, carrot, one potato (cut in half), bay leaf, and salt, and bring to a boil. Cut the second potato in ½-inch cubes, add to the pot. Cover, lower the heat, and simmer for about 20 minutes. When the halved potato and the carrot are tender, remove them, mash with a fork, and set them aside. Remove the bay leaf, and continue cooking the beans at a low boil until done (20 to 40 minutes).

Mince to a paste the salt pork, onion, garlic, sage, parsley, and celery, and sauté in the olive oil until golden. Add the sautéed minced flavorings and the reserved mashed carrot and potato to the soup, stir well, and cook for a few minutes longer. Serve hot or at room temperature, garnished with a dribble of extra-virgin olive oil.

Bean and Cabbage Soup

Minestra di borlotti e cavolo

Soak the beans overnight, or bring them to a boil in abundant lightly salted water, boil for 2 minutes, and let cool. Then bring back to a boil and simmer again until tender.

Trim the cabbage of any broken outer leaves, cut out and discard the core, and cut the remaining leaves in thin strips.

Boil the cabbage in enough salted water to cover for 5 minutes. Drain and rinse in cold water, and set aside.

Mince to a paste the onion, leek, carrot, celery, parsley, and salt pork. Sauté with the olive oil in a soup pot until golden and limp. Add the drained cabbage and cook, stirring, for 1 to 2 minutes. Add enough water to cover (about 4 cups), then add the sliced potato. Add the salt and pepper to taste, cover, and bring to a boil. Lower the heat and simmer until the potatoes are tender.

Slowly add the beef broth, return the soup to a boil, and add the beans and the uncooked rice. Cook until the rice is tender, about 13 to 15 minutes.

Serve, adding a generous sprinkling of Parmesan cheese to each bowl, and additional freshly ground pepper to taste.

1 cup Roman beans (borlotti), uncooked

1 small cabbage (2 to 2½ pounds approximate)

1 small onion

1 leek, white part only

1 small carrot

1 celery rib

6 to 7 sprigs flat-leaf parsley

3 ounces lean salt pork

2 tablespoons olive oil

1 small potato, peeled and sliced thin

Salt

Pepper

4 cups beef broth

¼ cup short- or medium-grain rice

6 tablespoons grated Parmesan cheese

Rice and Bean Soup

Ris e fasui

1 garlic clove

1 small onion

1 celery rib

2 tablespoons fresh flat-leaf
parsley, chopped

2 ounces lean salt pork

3 ounces mortadella

4 tablespoons olive oil

3 plum tomatoes, peeled and
chopped, or 2 tablespoons
tomato paste

2 cups canned red kidney beans,
undrained

8 cups hot water

1½ cups long-grain rice

3 to 4 tablespoons grated
Parmesan cheese

Mince the garlic, onion, celery, parsley, salt pork, and mortadella. In a soup pot, sauté the mince in the olive oil until golden and limp. Stir in the tomatoes. Cook for 2 to 3 minutes, then add the beans and their canning water. Bring to a low boil and cook for another 2 to 3 minutes. Add the water, bring to a boil, stir in the rice, and boil gently for about 14 minutes, or until the rice is tender. Serve with a sprinkling of grated Parmesan cheese.

Liguria

Genoese Minestrone with Pesto
Minestrone genovese al pesto

Linguini Soup
Minestra di bavette

Greens and Garlic Soup
Zuppa di verdure all'agliata

Stuffed Lettuce in Broth
Minestra di lattughe ripiene

Chickpea Soup
Zuppa di ceci

Chickpea, Bean, and Barley Soup
Mes-ciua

Ligurian Fish Soup—Cioppino
Ciuppin

Liguria

~

Seen from the sea, Liguria appears to be a huge natural amphitheater. Facing south, the sickle-shaped coastline climbs rapidly from the shore toward the tall mountain chain that protects it from northern winds. Alps and Apennines join in a mountainous embrace that entraps the warm breezes of the Ligurian Sea, letting the whole region enjoy a semipermanent spring. Even the clouds are kept at bay by the mountains, and the clear sky is mirrored in the many hues of the blue gulf. Romantic poets, from their vantage points of San Remo, Portofino, Santa Margherita, and Rapallo, have sung of its beauty.

The coastline is split into two rivieras, and Genoa, capital of Liguria, straddles the two: The western Riviera di Ponente begins where the French Cote d'Azur ends at the rocky spur of Ponte San Luigi, only a stone's throw from glitzy Monaco/Monte Carlo. The eastern Riviera di Levante leaves Genoa, stopping after about 94 miles at Lerici, at the edge of Tuscany, shortly after the green, perpendicular cliffs of Cinque Terre. In between, squeezed by mountains and sea, little growing soil is left in this natural greenhouse, and most of it is collected on terraces. Whatever grows, or is nursed and prodded to grow, has an enhanced character, a concentrate of all the humors cajoled from the earth: Man, land, and climate join forces to create the tastiest of produce. Even the flowers, with carnations leading the parade (they are a major local industry), seem to be more intensely scented and colored.

The Ligurians' parsimonious and shrewd administration of their goods is a necessary, sophisticated ingenuity. Here, where the majestic Mediterranean pine trees grow side by side with gnarled, centuries-old olive trees and intensely aromatic herbs, a Ligurian, in a stroke of genius, cautiously balanced pine nuts, olive oil, native basil, and garlic and, with mortar and pestle, pounded and squeezed their very essence into pesto.

The old adage *"far di necessità, virtù"*—from necessity, virtue—well applies to Ligurian gastronomy. Well known is the Ligurian ability to get the most out of a sea catch, as exemplified by their *ciuppin,* where even the bones, heads, and tails of the fish are cooked, squeezed, and sieved to make the classic fish soup; or a *cappon magro,* a construction of fish, sea biscuits (more frequently, dried-out old bread), and vegetables balanced to make a one-dish meal. This innate respect for all that the land offers appears in immaculately clean greengrocer stores and market stalls and the care given to their displays. The vegetables' juxtaposition of colors and shapes are like colors on an artist's palette. Each item is lined up in its crate to emphasize its best features, positioned so that its color catches the best light. Even on an overcast or rainy day, a Ligurian open-air market appears blessed with sunshine. There is no hurry in the customers: They stop and go from display to display in search of inspiration, letting the market dictate the menu for the day.

It is a shopping and cooking philosophy very much alive in the southeastern end of Liguria, the Cinque Terre. Somewhat removed from the glamour of the Rivieras, it could very well represent, in concentrate form, the character of the whole region and its cuisine.

Where the Apennine Mountains leave off courting the Ligurian coastline and finally plunge into the Tyrrhenean Sea, there stand the five villages that make up the "Five Lands." Strung along twenty miles, Corniglia, Manarola, Monterosso, Riomaggiore, and Vernazza look painted on the mountain walls that emerge straight up from the coast. The Cinque Terre can be reached by ferryboat from Sestri or Lerici, or by railroad: The train, going in and out of tunnels like a giant's needle, stitches the five villages to the rest of Liguria, and it in turn to the rest of Italy. The whole land looks as if scratched by horizontal lines, the work of a huge hand's nails. Only from close by, one realizes that these are steep terraces carved out of the cliffs' walls, only two or three feet wide.

In the traditional cuisine, only what grows locally and what is fished from the reluctant sea ends in the pot. And a fragrant pot it is: Basil, marjoram, mint, rosemary, oregano, and, above all, garlic—all generously used local herbs—spice up and give the unique Ligurian fragrance to any dish. Exposed to sea-moist breezes and protected from chilly inland winds, the terraced vineyards produce the strong, sweet Sciacchetrà and the famous white, dry, scented Cinqueterre wine. Experts say these wines seem invented to accompany the local food; others say that their fame comes from their scarcity: So little is produced that only a few bottles leave the area.

Perhaps those few bottles are fine where they are: where food and wine take advantage of the special chemistry of sea and mountain air. The chemistry of Liguria.

Genoese Minestrone with Pesto

Minestrone genovese al pesto

The addition of pesto is what makes this minestrone special. It is excellent when made with the freshest vegetables, but it is also very good when canned or frozen ingredients are used. The type and quantities of vegetables may be the cook's choice, and the ones listed are mere suggestions. To take advantage of the largest number of vegetables available, the soup should be made in a large batch: Use what is immediately needed and save the rest. If the soup is to be eaten in installments, divide the amount of pasta proportionately and cook it in the portion of minestrone that you are serving—it loses its texture if reheated.

Mince the celery, 1 onion, 1 carrot, the salt pork, and the basil. Sauté the mince in a soup pot in the olive oil until the salt pork is translucent and the seasonings are limp.

Slice the 2 remaining carrots in thin rounds and add, with the diced potatoes, leeks, tomatoes, zucchini, and escarole, to the soup pot. Add the water and salt, and stir.

Bring the pot to a boil, and cover. Lower the heat, and simmer for about 20 to 30 minutes, or until the vegetables are cooked but still firm. Return the pot to a boil, add the pasta and the beans, and cook 8 minutes or until the pasta is done. Turn off the heat and let rest a few minutes.

Stir in the pesto and mix well. Serve warm, topped with the grated Parmesan and pecorino cheeses. Or mix the cheeses in the soup, allow to cool, and serve at room temperature, with a dribbling of extra-virgin olive oil over each portion.

1 celery stalk with leaves, minced

2 onions

3 carrots, peeled

3 ounces (3 to 4 slices approximate) lean salt pork

4 fresh basil leaves

4 tablespoons olive oil

2 potatoes, peeled and diced

2 leeks, white part only, sliced in thin rounds

2 tomatoes, peeled and quartered

2 zucchini, cubed

1 handful escarole, cut in bite-size pieces

(Cont.)

9 cups warm water

3½ teaspoons salt

*2 cups small macaroni (tubettini,
shells,* ditalini)

*1 cup cooked kidney beans, fresh
or canned*

*4 tablespoons pesto (see below),
or to taste*

*2 tablespoons grated Parmesan
cheese*

*2 tablespoons grated pecorino
Romano cheese*

PESTO:

Pesto means "pounded," hence anything that is pounded long enough could be called a pesto. But in the Italian—and absolutely in the Ligurian—food lexicon, it means only one pesto, made with only *fresh basil* as the leading ingredient. All the rest are pesto impostors. There is, nonetheless, some freedom in the proportions of the ingredients—you may want to adjust them to your personal taste.

   If you do not have a mortar and pestle, this is the best reason to get one.

*2 cups loosely packed fresh basil
leaves*

2 to 3 garlic cloves

½ teaspoon salt

3 ounces pine nuts

*2 tablespoons freshly grated
pecorino Romano cheese*

½ cup extra-virgin olive oil

Salt

Place the basil, garlic, salt, and pine nuts in the mortar bowl, and mash and pound until you have a pretty smooth paste. (You may use a food processor, but do it where no Ligurian can see you. . . .) Add the cheese to the paste and stir well, then add the olive oil. Add salt to taste. The final pesto should be spoonable, of a consistency similar to thick yogurt. One tablespoon goes a long way: When used on pasta, it is diluted with some warm pasta-cooking water.

Notes: Adjust the amount of garlic to your taste: Some pestos are very garlicky. For a less sharp garlic flavor, soak the cloves overnight in half a cup of milk.

The amount of pine nuts may be cut down by one ounce and replaced by the same amount of walnut meats.

The amount of cheese may be split between Romano and Parmesan.

Since pesto keeps well in the refrigerator, it is convenient to make two or three batches at a time.

To the basil leaves, you may add 2 to 3 fresh spinach leaves, or the leaves of 3 to 4 sprigs of Italian flat-leaf pars-ley: They give a deeper green color to the pesto.

Linguini Soup

Minestra di bavette

2 quarts chicken or beef broth

9 to 10 ounces linguini (bavette)

6 sprigs fresh marjoram (see
   Note), chopped, or ¼ teaspoon
   dried oregano

3 eggs

Salt

Freshly ground white pepper

4 tablespoons grated Parmesan
   cheese, plus more as needed for
   garnish

In a soup pot, bring the broth to a boil and add the linguini along with the marjoram. When it returns to a boil,
stir the pasta, and cook about 8 minutes, or until the pasta
is al dente—cooked but with a bit of bite to it.

In a bowl, beat the eggs well, with half the Parmesan
cheese, salt and pepper to your taste, and 1 to 2 tablespoons of the broth.

When the pasta is ready, add the egg-cheese mixture to
the broth, stir, and ladle into soup plates. Top with additional Parmesan cheese, if desired.

Note: If fresh marjoram is not available, wait until the
season brings it to your garden, as dried marjoram does
not work as well. Using a "pinch" of dried oregano will
just make it.

Greens and Garlic Soup

Zuppa di verdure all'agliata

One of the elements that distinguishes the Ligurian cuisine from other regional cuisines is its generous use of, and love for, garlic. A Ligurian would consider conservative the amount of garlic given in the following recipe; it may be adjusted upward—or downward—depending on the amount of Ligurian blood running in your veins.

In a soup pot over medium heat, sauté the onion in the olive oil until the onion is limp.

Add the cabbage, Bibb lettuce, Swiss chard, turnip, celery, carrots, potatoes, and tomatoes. Add salt and pepper, and cook and stir until the vegetables are slightly limp and the tomato and potato pieces softened.

Add the hot broth to the soup pot and continue cooking for about 15 minutes. Add the peas and cook until they are tender, about 5 minutes.

Meanwhile, mince to a paste the parsley and the garlic, and stir into the pot.

Taste for salt and adjust if needed. Cook for another few minutes, until all the vegetables are tender. Place slices of toast in each serving bowl, and ladle the soup over them. Serve with grated Parmesan cheese.

⅓ cup olive oil

1 medium onion, sliced fine

½ head savoy cabbage (1 pound approximate), cored

5 to 6 leaves Bibb lettuce

5 to 6 leaves Swiss chard

1 turnip, sliced thin

2 celery ribs, leaves removed, sliced thin

2 carrots, peeled and sliced thin

3 small potatoes, peeled and cubed

3 plum tomatoes, peeled, seeded, and chopped

1½ teaspoons salt

Freshly ground white pepper

7 to 8 cups vegetable broth (page 254), heated

1 cup frozen peas

(Cont.)

6 sprigs flat-leaf parsley, stems removed

5 to 6 garlic cloves

6 slices Italian-style white bread, oven-toasted and rubbed with garlic

Grated Parmesan cheese

Stuffed Lettuce in Broth

Minestra di lattughe ripiene

These filled lettuce packets, served in broth, are a modern vegetarian version of a traditional dish that uses less esoteric ingredients (calf brains, veal udder, etc.) than the old one.

1 medium eggplant (8 to 10 ounces)

3 garlic cloves

3 tablespoons olive oil

2 celery ribs, cut in ½-inch slices

1 onion, chopped coarsely

½ green or red bell pepper, chopped coarsely, seeds discarded

1 small zucchini, cut in thin rounds

½ teaspoon salt

Cut the eggplant in 1-inch-thick slices, sprinkle freely with salt, and place in a colander for 15 to 20 minutes so that their bitter moisture can drain away.

In a sizeable pan, sauté the garlic in the olive oil over medium heat until the garlic is golden. Depending on your appreciation of garlic, either remove it or mash it with a fork into the oil. Add the celery and the onion to the pan, and when they begin to wilt, add the bell pepper. Rinse the eggplant rounds under cold water, cube them, and add to the pan, with the zucchini rounds. Add the salt and Tabasco sauce, and increase the heat. Add the wine and the vinegar, and stir. Lower the heat, cover the pan, and cook, stirring occasionally, for 10 minutes, or until the vegetables are cooked but still firm. Remove from heat and allow to cool. When cold, transfer the vegetables with a slotted spoon to a cutting board or to the bowl of a food processor. Reserve the cooking liquid. Chop the vegetables coarsely, so that the mixture still has some texture. Add the eggs, Romano cheese, and enough bread crumbs to give it a reasonably solid, spoonable consistency. Add salt to taste.

Take, without breaking them, 12 Bibb lettuce leaves, retaining as much of the white stem as possible. Plunge them, one at a time, into a pot of boiling water for only a few seconds, to make them pliable. Allow to drain and place them on a work surface. Scoop ½ of the filler onto the leaf center. Fold it to enclose the filler. Pull the lower edge of the leaf barely over the filler; fold the left and right edges in the same way; then fold down the upper edge to make a tight packet. If necessary, tie with a white cotton thread to keep it shut. Set aside, and continue with the other leaves.

In a soup pot, bring the broth almost to the boiling point. With a slotted spoon, lower the lettuce packets into it. When they are warmed through, about 1 to 2 minutes, scoop them out, and place two in each serving dish. Ladle the hot broth over them and serve with a good sprinkling of grated Romano cheese.

1 teaspoon Tabasco sauce

¼ cup dry white wine

1 tablespoon wine vinegar

2 eggs

3 tablespoons grated pecorino Romano cheese, plus more as needed for garnish

3 to 4 tablespoons unflavored bread crumbs, or more as needed

12 outer leaves of Bibb or iceberg lettuce

7 cups beef broth

Chickpea Soup

Zuppa di ceci

4 ounces prosciutto, or lean
  salt pork

1 small onion

2 garlic cloves

1 small carrot

1 white celery rib

1 ounce dried porcini mushrooms,
  soaked and well drained

3 anchovy filets, chopped

3 tablespoons olive oil

3 to 4 Swiss chard leaves with
  stems, chopped coarsely

3 tablespoons tomato paste

1 cup warm water

4 cups canned chickpeas,
  undrained

7 cups chicken broth, warmed

Salt

Freshly ground pepper

6 to 12 slices Italian-style white
  bread, oven-toasted

Mince the prosciutto with the onion, 1 garlic clove, carrot, celery, mushrooms, and anchovies. In a soup pot, sauté the mince in the olive oil over low heat. When the mince has taken on color, add the chard. Stir, and cook until the chard is barely wilted. Dilute the tomato paste in the warm water. Add the chickpeas with their liquid, and the tomato liquid, to the soup pot. Add chicken broth, and salt and pepper to taste. Bring the pot to a boil, then lower the heat and simmer for about 15 minutes. Scoop out some of the chickpeas and mash to a paste, then return them to the pot.

Rub the toasted bread with the remaining garlic clove, divide among the soup plates, and pour the soup over the bread. Serve immediately.

Chickpea, Bean, and Barley Soup

Mes-ciua

Here is a soup that was used for centuries, put away for a time, and now has been brought back for those who wish to revive tradition. The name, in dialect, means a "bit of everything," putting together what is available in a larder running low. It is loaded with protein, its flavor heightened by freshly ground pepper and good olive oil.

In one pan, combine the chickpeas and barley with enough water to cover. In another, place the beans with enough water to cover. Soak both pans overnight.

In a soup pot, combine the chickpeas and barley with 1 teaspoon of the salt, the rosemary, 2 tablespoons of the olive oil, and 4 cups water. Bring to a boil and then simmer, covered, for about 30 to 40 minutes, or until the barley is tender.

In a separate pot combine the beans, ½ teaspoon of the salt, 2 tablespoons of the olive oil, the garlic, and about 3 cups of water. Bring to a boil and then simmer for about 20 or 30 minutes, or until beans are tender. Retrieve and discard the garlic. (Cooking times may vary with the quality of the dry ingredients.)

Scoop the beans from their cooking water, reserving the liquid, and add them to the chickpeas pot. Add enough of the reserved cooking water (if necessary) to have about 7 to 8 cups of *mes-ciua* in the pot.

Add salt to taste. Cook at a low boil for another 10 minutes. Retrieve and discard the rosemary. The soup should

1 cup dried chickpeas

½ cup pearl barley

1 cup dried Great Northern (cannellini) beans

2 teaspoons salt

1 sprig fresh rosemary, or 1 tablespoon dry rosemary tied in a piece of cheesecloth

4 tablespoons olive oil

1 garlic clove

4 to 6 tablespoons extra-virgin olive oil (approximate)

Freshly ground pepper

be reasonably dense; if not, mash some of it with a wooden spoon, or if too thick, add more of the reserved cooking liquid.

Serve immediately, topped to taste with extra-virgin olive oil and freshly ground pepper.

Ligurian Fish Soup—Cioppino

Ciuppin

Established as "cioppino" in San Francisco by its large contingent of Ligurian immigrants, the name is one of the rare cases in which an Italian word, traveling abroad, acquires a vowel instead of losing one. The original version is a thick, smooth fish potage; in the Cinque Terre, south of Genoa, where they claim the paternity for *ciuppin,* the preparation is so thick that it may be used as a sauce for pasta.

As in many fish soups, the larger the variety of whole small fish, the more successful the *ciuppin.* For a richer version, shrimp, squid, and lobster meat may be added.

FOR THE BROTH:

1 onion

1 carrot, peeled

1 celery rib, trimmed

2 to 3 garlic cloves, or more if desired

2 tablespoons flat-leaf parsley, chopped

4 flat anchovy filets

⅓ teaspoon salt

Chop the onion, carrot, celery, garlic, parsley, and anchovies. In a soup pot, sauté the chopped mixture, the salt, and cayenne in the olive oil until the vegetables are limp. Add the wine, stir, and allow to evaporate a bit. Add the undrained tomatoes and mash them coarsely with a fork. Add the water, and stir. Add salt and pepper to taste, and bring to a boil. Simmer, uncovered, for 15 to 20 minutes.

Cut the small fish in chunks (heads and tails included), and add to the simmering broth. (If using fish filets and racks, cut the filets and racks in chunks and add to the simmering broth.)

Bring to a boil, then reduce the heat and let cook for about 20 minutes, or until the fish is thoroughly cooked and the flesh falls off the bones. Allow to cool.

Place a colander over another soup pot, pour the contents of the first pot into the colander, and with a wooden spoon, press and squeeze the cooked fish through the colander. If needed, repeat the process with a tighter-mesh sieve to obtain a reasonably smooth and thin fish puree.

Stir and simmer the puree. It should have the consistency of heavy cream. If too liquid, allow to reduce a bit; if too thick, stir in a little warm water.

While the *ciuppin* is simmering, toast the bread slices, rub them very lightly with a garlic clove, and divide among warmed serving dishes. Ladle the soup over the bread and serve.

Optional: Add the olive oil to a sauté pan over high heat. When the oil is hot, add the squid and shrimp and sauté until the shrimp takes on a coral color. Add the cooked lobster meat and the wine, cover the pan, and swirl the contents around for 15 to 20 seconds. Remove from heat, uncover, and stir the pan contents into the *ciuppin.*

¼ *teaspoon ground cayenne pepper*

¼ *cup olive oil*

1 *cup dry white wine*

2 *cups (28-ounce can) canned Italian-style tomatoes, undrained*

6 to 7 *cups warm water*

Salt

Pepper

12 *slices baguette-style bread, cut on the diagonal*

FOR THE FISH:

5 to 6 *pounds assorted whole fish (cleaned but with heads and tails on), such as sea bass, black sea bass, gray mullet, snapper, porgy, whiting, sea robin*

2½ to 3 *pounds of firm-fleshed fish filets, such as halibut, monkfish, haddock, grouper, and 3 to 4 pounds fish heads and bones (called "racks" in the trade)*

THE FOLLOWING IS OPTIONAL:

2 *tablespoons olive oil*

¼ *pound squid, cleaned and cut in rings*

¼ *pound small shrimp, shelled and deveined*

Cooked meat of 1 lobster, cut in chunks

¼ *cup dry white wine*

Emilia–Romagna

Soup in the Style of Bologna
Zuppa alla bolognese

Soup of Pasta Bits
Malfattini romagnoli

Eggs and Rice Soup
Ris e tritura

Modena's Egg and Spinach Soup
Zuppa di spinaci alla modenese

Bologna's Bean Soup
Maritati

Rice Quenelles in Broth
Chenelle di riso in brodo

Cheese Cappelletti
Cappelletti di magro

Chicken, Mortadella, and Lentil Soup
Zuppa ricca di lenticchie

Emilia–Romagna

S outh of the river Po and north of Tuscany lies Emilia–Romagna. By square miles, it is the sixth in size among the Italian regions. Prior to the unification of Italy, it was the region with the greatest number of independent city-states, duchies, principalities, counties, and Pontifical Legations. Perhaps because of its geographical position and climate the region has always been a perfect ground for many cultures to grow and flourish.

In Villanova di Castenaso, a village six miles outside Bologna, artifacts brought to the surface attest that Indo-European man, during his slow migration west, stopped and made his home in this area during the Bronze Age. He was followed in the Iron Age by the Italics (ancestors of the Italians and fathers of the Romanic languages), who established Villanova as an important agricultural and metal production center—important enough to give its name to the Villanovian Civilization. They merged in the sixth century B.C. with the Northern Etruscans, and these, in the middle of the fourth century B.C., fell under the domination of Gauls who, in turn, around the second century B.C. were defeated by the Romans. The Romans, as was their habit, founded a town and called it Bononia, today's Bologna, the capital of the region. The road that, straight as an arrow, connects Rimini on the Adriatic Sea with the Po Valley and Milan is named for the Roman consul who ordered its construction. The Aemilian Way gave its name to the region, Emilia. With the waning of the Romans, the Byzantines took over and imposed their law and culture, leaving their artistic mark in the unrivaled mosaics of Ravenna.

In the Renaissance, the powerful, gilded courts of Ferrara, Modena, Parma, Piacenza, Rimini, and Forlì cosseted and embraced culture and the arts and—enriched by the lifestyles of the French, Spanish, Austrian, and Pontifical courts—used them to project power and exuberant vitality. Like magnets, the cities attracted fashion, beauty, and wealth from all points of the compass. All the seven arts blossomed, as did architecture, commerce, and gastronomy, shaping the character of the region and its people.

This vitality is best represented by the attitude of its citizens and can be described as *gioia di vivere,* zest for life. The Emiliani–Romagnoli exude a sense of purposeful enjoyment of life. They ignore half measures. The pulsating blood can be felt in the paintings of Caravaggio and Guido Reni, in the music of Verdi, in the scientific zeal of Galvani, in the intensity of Rimini's Paolo and Francesca's love. It can be recognized in the daring technology of the Ferrari and the Maserati and the Lamborghini, in the vibrancy of Pavarotti's voice, in the poetry of Pascoli and Carducci, in the ingenuity of Marconi, in the artistry of Toscanini, in the imagination of Fellini, in the uncompromisingly lusty cuisine. Walk the streets of any of its cities, and you will find this zest contagious: Life in Emilia–Romagna happens in public. Alleys, streets, avenues, and squares are all a common living room: It is there that, rain or shine, the commerce of life happens. It is there that people walk and mingle and talk and shop and do business, congregate and argue and laugh. Even the architecture of the cities is tailored for this all-hours, all-weather life: Every building is contoured by vaulted porticoes, shaded by day, well-lit by night. In Bologna alone there are twenty-two miles of porticoes, a single city's greatest number in the entire world, and you can go from one end of town to the other without the need of a parasol or of an umbrella.

The University of Bologna, approaching its 910th birthday, is the oldest continuously active university in existence, the first and original Alma Mater Studiorum. It is in homage to its university that Bologna has been known through the ages as La Dotta, "the learned." With equal value and status, Bologna is known as La Grassa, which stands not only for lover of gastronomy but also of all that is plentiful and good, lively, and lusty.

Considering the high achievement and economic level of the region—the "golden triangle" of Modena, Reggio Emilia, and Bologna delimits the richest area in Italy—one would expect a frenetic workaholic pace. Instead, a visitor will be surprised by the quiet, almost lackadaisical tempo in the heart of any of the big cities or charming small towns and villages. In the birthplace of superfast cars, the bicycle is the most common way of transportation: Close to lunch and dinner time, the streets become flowing rivers of bicyclists, young and old, heading home, one supposes, to a waiting, well-stocked table.

The importance of food in the texture of life in Emilia–Romagna is exemplified by one of the region's creations. Where else in the world would a lovestruck cook, inspired by his inamorata's anatomy, shape from thin pasta and spiced forcemeat a tasty morsel and call it "Venus' belly-button"? Only misplaced prudery renamed that delight a *tortellino* or *cappelletto,* as they are now known the world over. One of the region's gastronomic specialties is Mortadella di Bologna, the huge sausage that, once landed in America, becomes simply bologna and is commonly called—you guessed it—baloney. Is there anyone who does not know of that layered, edible wonder called lasagne? Or of *Parmigiano* cheese, ravioli, prosciutto di Parma, Bolognese meat sauce, egg-pasta fettuccine, Modena *cotechino* salami. . . . The list is so extensive that it is impossible to name any of the region's cities, towns, or villages and not come up with a specialty.

Our latest pilgrimage throughout Emilia–Romagna was wisely interspersed with gastronomic stops, and never a single menu was repeated. From agnolotti with a spinach-and-cheese filling in Ferrara to tortelloni with pumpkin filling in Parma, from a *brodetto* fish soup in Rimini to a *cotechino*-and-lentil soup in Modena, from the lightest of grilled *trippa* in Forlì to *pappardelle* with salmon and asparagus tips in Busseto or *piadine* in Ravenna . . . we had it all.

The trip ended in Modena—land of my ancestors—and at dinner our host, my cousin, quoted a regional old saw: Lifting in a toast a glass of ruby red, dry and sparkling real Lambrusco, "*A tavola,*" he said, "*non si invecchia!*" "One doesn't grow old at table!"

By that old saying, we did not age a minute during our last ten days in town.

Soup in the Style of Bologna

Zuppa alla bolognese

6 eggs

4 ounces grated Parmesan cheese

1 cup semolina flour (see Note)

Dash of freshly grated nutmeg

Salt

4 ounces mortadella

4 tablespoons unsalted butter

7 cups beef broth

Preheat the oven to 400°F.

Separate the eggs and put the yolks, Parmesan cheese, ¾ cup of the flour, nutmeg, and salt in a bowl. Mix well. Mince the mortadella very fine, melt 3 tablespoons of the butter, and add both to the yolk-flour mixture.

Beat the egg whites until holding a peak and fold them slowly into the mixture to form a smooth batter. Do not overwork it.

Butter an 8- or 9-inch baking dish with the remaining 1 tablespoon of the butter and dust it with the remaining ¼ cup of the flour. Spoon the mixture into the baking dish and bake for 10 to 15 minutes, or until a cake tester comes out clean.

Allow to cool, and cut into small cubes (crouton-size) or small triangles.

In a soup pot, bring the broth to boil, add the cubes, and cook for about 3 minutes, or until the cubes are heated through. Serve immediately.

Note: The semolina flour may be replaced with finely ground corn flour.

Soup of Pasta Bits

Malfattini romagnoli

For the pasta bits:

If using homemade egg pasta, mix as in the recipe, adding the freshly grated nutmeg. After the pasta is kneaded and smooth, roll it out to a sheet ⅛-inch thick, using either a long, thin Italian-style rolling pin or a pasta machine. Cut into 3 × 5-inch rectangles, flour lightly on both sides, and let dry for 30 minutes on clean kitchen towels or floured cookie sheets. Once dry enough so that the pasta pieces don't stick, chop them haphazardly with a very sharp knife. The resulting pasta bits, *malfattini* ("poorly done"), should be about as big as large grains of cooked rice. Once all the pasta is cut, spread it out on a dry surface to dry completely. Save any small crumbs resulting from the cuttings. They should end up in the soup too, and make it even thicker.

If using commercial egg noodles, place them in a clean kitchen towel, fold the towel to cover the pasta (or put the pasta in a plastic bag) and roll and pound with a rolling pin until the pasta has been broken into suitable bits.

For the soup:

In a soup pot, heat the olive oil and the butter, and sauté the celery, carrot, and onion over medium heat until vegetables are golden and limp, about 15 minutes.

Wash the greens thoroughly; put in another pot with only the water that clings to the leaves. Cook/steam them over medium heat until tender. Drain thoroughly, cool slightly, and chop coarsely.

1 two-egg batch homemade pasta (pages 256–260) with ¼ teaspoon freshly grated nutmeg added, or 8 ounces dried pasta

4 tablespoons olive oil

4 tablespoons unsalted butter

1 celery rib, trimmed and chopped

1 large carrot, peeled and chopped

1 small onion, chopped

1 pound fresh greens (a mixture of spinach, lettuce, romaine, and endive, if possible; otherwise, all spinach will do)

2 tablespoons tomato paste

8 cups water

2 teaspoons salt

4 to 5 tablespoons grated Parmesan cheese

Add the chopped greens, tomato paste, water, and salt to the sautéed vegetables. Stir, bring to a boil, lower the heat, and simmer about 10 minutes.

Return the soup to a boil, stir in the *malfattini* and its crumbs, and continue cooking until the pasta is tender, about 5 minutes, stirring occasionally.

Serve immediately, topped with the Parmesan cheese.

Eggs and Rice Soup

Ris e tritura

This soup is an easy *minestra* that appears, with variations, in several other regional cuisines. The common element is the beaten eggs stirred into a boiling liquid. The additional ingredients change with the region and give a different accent to the soups.

8 cups beef broth

¾ cup rice

6 eggs

6 tablespoons freshly grated Parmesan cheese, plus more as needed for garnish

½ teaspoon salt

½ teaspoon freshly grated nutmeg

In a soup pot, bring the beef broth to a boil. Add the rice, cover, and cook at a very low boil for about 12 minutes.

Meanwhile, in a bowl combine the eggs, cheese, salt, and nutmeg, and beat well. Stir the mixture into the broth and let the soup cook, stirring constantly, for a minute or two, until the rice is completely done.

Serve the soup with additional grated Parmesan cheese.

Modena's Egg and Spinach Soup

Zuppa di spinaci alla modenese

Wash and rinse the spinach well and shake it dry. In a covered pot, cook the spinach with the salt and only the water that clings to its leaves. Drain the cooked spinach well and, when cool enough, squeeze dry and mince fine.

Melt the butter in a large saucepan, add the spinach, and sauté briefly. Remove from heat, let cool, and put the spinach in a bowl.

In a second bowl, beat together the eggs, Parmesan cheese, nutmeg, and pepper, to taste. Add the mixture to the minced spinach, and mix well.

In a soup pot bring the broth to a boil, add the spinach-egg mixture, and stir thoroughly. Leave over the heat briefly—do not overcook. Divide the toasted slices of bread or the croutons among the serving dishes and top with the hot soup.

1½ pounds fresh spinach

½ teaspoon salt

2 tablespoons unsalted butter

4 eggs

4 to 5 tablespoons grated Parmesan cheese

Dash of nutmeg

Freshly ground pepper

7 cups broth

6 to 12 slices of Italian-style white bread, oven-toasted, or croutons

Bologna's Bean Soup

Maritati

Maritati means "wedded," and in regional culinary terms, it stands for the supposedly happy joining of two elements, generally a soup and something else. In this case it is a bean soup and *ditalini,* or short pasta. It can be substituted by *quadrucci,* tiny squares of egg pasta, or by commercial egg noodles broken into small pieces.

2 to 3 garlic cloves

2 tablespoons olive oil

2 tablespoons unsalted butter

2 teaspoons minced flat-leaf parsley

2 cups plum tomatoes, peeled and crushed

12 ounces canned kidney beans, undrained

8 to 9 cups water

8 ounces ditalini

Salt

Freshly ground pepper

Grated Parmesan cheese

In a soup pot, sauté the garlic cloves in the olive oil and butter until well browned. Remove and discard the garlic. Add the minced parsley, tomatoes, and the undrained beans. Simmer for about 10 minutes, then scoop out and mash about half the beans. Return the mashed beans to the pot, add the water, and stir well.

Bring the soup to a boil. Add the *ditalini,* and cook about 8 to 10 minutes, or until the pasta is tender.

Serve with a generous amount of grated Parmesan cheese.

Rice Quenelles in Broth

Chenelle di riso in brodo

The Italicized *chenelle* is an obvious sign of the French influence in the rich, cosmopolitan courts of Renaissance Emilia–Romagna, when emulation of foreign gastronomies—especially French—was considered a sign of elegance and cultural refinement.

Boil the veal in 4 cups lightly salted water for about 15 minutes. Drain well and allow to cool.

Cook the rice in 2 cups boiling salted water for 16 minutes, or until very well done. Drain well and allow to cool.

In a small saucepan, briefly sauté the chicken livers in the butter. Place the veal, rice, livers, egg yolks, salt, pepper, and nutmeg in a food processor with the steel blade in place and process until a homogeneous, rollable paste has been achieved. If too soft, add a little grated Parmesan cheese.

Flour your hands and roll the resulting paste on a lightly floured work surface into cylinders of about ½-inch diameter (about finger size). Cut into 2-inch lengths. Let *chenelle* rest for 15 minutes.

In a soup pot, bring the broth to a simmer. With a slotted spoon lower a few *chenelle* at a time into the broth; scoop them out as soon as they float to the surface. Divide them among the serving dishes, ladle warm broth over them, and serve.

¾ pound veal shoulder or veal stew meat, cubed

½ cup short- or medium-grain rice

2 chicken livers

½ tablespoon unsalted butter

2 egg yolks

Salt

Pepper

Dash of freshly ground nutmeg

Freshly grated Parmesan cheese

1 cup all-purpose flour

7 cups beef broth

Cheese Cappelletti

Cappelletti di magro

Cappelletti literally means "little hats," and that, in fact, is what these small cheese-filled squares of pasta look like once they have been carefully twisted and turned. When we moved from Italy, no one in America sold cappelletti, as far as we knew, so we made our own to entertain our American relatives.

Cappelletti may be made at any time and then frozen for future use: Place single layers of the filled pasta on aluminum foil in the freezer until well frozen, when they may easily be put in a self-sealing plastic bag.

Cappelletti may also be purchased in most supermarkets. Use about two ounces—a nice handful—per serving.

4 ounces soft cheese, such as
  Fontina or Muenster

4 ounces ricotta

3 tablespoons grated Parmesan
  cheese, plus more as needed for
  garnish

Dash of freshly grated nutmeg

1 egg

1 two-egg batch of homemade
  pasta, (pages 256–260)

7 to 8 cups chicken broth

Place the soft cheese, ricotta, Parmesan, nutmeg, and egg in a food processor with the steel blade in position, and mince until you have a paste. If the result is too soft, add a bit more Parmesan.

Form the fresh pasta into cappelletti.

Bring the broth to a boil and add the cappelletti a few at a time. Return the broth to a boil, lower the heat, and cook gently for about 8 to 10 minutes, or for 2 minutes after the cappelletti float to the surface. Serve with grated Parmesan cheese.

Chicken, Mortadella, and Lentil Soup

Zuppa ricca di lenticchie

Soak the dried lentils overnight (although a 2-hour soaking is sufficient) in enough water to cover. Drain the lentils and cook them at a low boil in salted water with the celery, carrot, and onion. When the lentils are almost cooked (15 minutes), add the mortadella cubes and cook until the lentils are done (another 8 to 10 minutes). Scoop out and dispose of celery, carrot, and onion, then drain the lentils, reserving ½ cup of the cooking water.

Bring the broth to a boil and add to it the lentil mixture. Add the cubed chicken and salt to taste; if too thick, add reserved water. Simmer for 2 to 3 minutes, and serve.

2½ cups dried lentils

6 cups water

1 teaspoon salt

1 celery rib, halved

1 small carrot

1 small onion, halved

4 ounces mortadella, cubed

7 cups chicken broth

1 breast of chicken, boiled, boned, and cubed

Salt

Toscana

Bread Soup
Minestra di pane

Potato Soup
Zuppa di patate

Cabbage Minestrone
Minestrone di cavolo

Tuscan Rice and Bean Soup
Minestra di riso e fagioli alla toscana

Livorno's Bean and Cabbage Soup
Bordatino

Bean and Cabbage "Reboiled" Soup
Ribollita

Grosseto's Mushroom and Egg "Cooked Water" Soup
Acquacotta

Egg and Marsala Soup
Cinestrata

Tomato Soup, Peasant Style
Pappa al pomodoro

Ricotta Green Dumplings in Broth
Gnocchi verdi di ricotta in brodo

Tuscan Fish Soup
Cacciucco

Toscana

I do not suggest you enter Tuscany on foot, but however you do it, do it slowly, not a step but a stop at a time. Then Tuscany will reward the attentive traveler and open up to you—hill after hill, beauty after beauty, surprise after surprise. It will be hard work and only the beginning: The moment you presume to have seen Tuscany, you will find a new and different one beyond the next bend, whichever road you take.

Coming from the north, old Route 65 leaves Bologna deliberately, straight at first, then climbing up in twists and turns, steady as a mountain mule, following the watershed of the Tosco-Emiliano Apennines. By the time you reach the Raticosa Pass, at three thousand feet, the air is thin and clear, and the breathing is easy: Emilia is behind, and Tuscany opens up ahead and below. Small villages go by, a few houses on each side of the road, one pasted on the side of the mountain, another rooted on the edge of the precipice. In one of them, between its signs reading "*Benvenuti!* Welcome!" and "*Arrivederci!* See you again!" there is a small church. It is very modest, with a spray of weedy flowers growing on the threshold of the weathered, wooden door. In its lunette is a ceramic bas-relief: a Madonna holding the Child. The delicate design, the cerulean blues, the creamy whites, the garland of fruits and flowers give it away as a Della Robbia work. Here? But is it? It doesn't matter. It is beautiful, even more so for appearing suddenly, unannounced. Compared to it, the great artworks you will encounter later, museumed and protected, will seem embalmed and mummified, a taxidermist's work. Here, in this unknown church of this unknown village, the perhaps Della Robbia—its brilliant highlights stolen from the open sky—is full of life.

Welcome to Tuscany.

Go on a few miles, and the high, green hills of the Muggello will glide into sets of lower hills and then lower again in different shades of green. Cared for and cultivated since the first day of Genesis, the landscape is a work of art in a land of artists. Soon the hills turn into wavy pastures and orderly farmland and vineyards. Don't be deceived, and go slowly—history hides behind every bump of the land. At the hamlet of Cafaggiolo, Michelozzo Michelozzi, the architect of Renaissance Florence, built a villa for the Medici. In its backyard Amerigo Vespucci, the navigator, planted a sequoia tree brought back from the land that bears his name. It is still there and growing.

In one of these pastures, it is said, Cimabue, master painter, discovered a young shepherd who, with a single stroke, drew a perfect circle on a field stone. He decided the boy deserved lessons; today, the master's name is obscured by the pupil's, Giotto. His house is still here, near the village of Vicchio, the same village where monk Fra Angelico, he of the spiritual and prolific brush, was born. Farther on, closer to Florence, you will encounter a farmhouse and then a few houses and a museum: It is Vinci, birthplace of—and forever associated with—Leonardo.

If you leave the Adriatic Sea at your back, to enter Tuscany you must cross the Apennines again. They are harsh and steep, and just over their peak, barely inside Tuscany and a short distance from each other, are the sources of two of the most fateful rivers in Italy: the Arno and the Tiber. They run south on parallel beds, searching for and reaching their sea, one at Pisa, the other near Rome. On the way they form what are considered two of the most beautiful valleys in Italy, the Val d'Arno and the Valle Tiberina.

On Tuscany's west, just before the Tyrrhenian Sea, are the Apuane. As mountains go, they are not terribly tall—about five thousand feet at their tallest—and their snow caps and white-streaked sides are not snow at all but marble, Carrara marble. To reach the quarries, few roads nose straight up and zigzag on the carved flanks of the mountains, at times piercing them, tunneling into rock, leaving one ravine behind to resurface in another. Travel is slow and difficult, to be negotiated curve by curve, quarry by quarry. What is not hard to do is to see these mountains as the marble womb that produced cathedrals, churches, synagogues, mosques, and pagan temples all around the world.

Just as every single piece of Tuscan landscape has its definite identity, impossible to describe with a single word or adjective, so is the makeup of the people. Any Tuscan will tell you that a single, homogeneous Tuscan character does not exist. He will tell you that a Fiorentino is as different from a Pisano as a Lucchese is from a Sienese, as they all are from everybody else. He will say so forcefully, convincingly. Do not believe it. It is a lie.

Tuscans are liars. His lie will not be a bashful excuse for truth; it will sound more like a boast, a challenge to the world to dare to question his veracity. You will seldom hear a Tuscan whisper: Whatever he has to say, he will say it forcefully, for everyone to hear.

The Tuscan has a mind as nimble as an Olympic sprinter, as agile as a jester, as difficult to hold as quicksilver. He will tell you he is the only real repository of the pure Italian language. But then, Tuscans do not use that language to communicate: They use it to engage in word duels, with feints and thrusts of witticisms as sharp as sabers and just as cutting.

The Tuscan loves laughter: His smile is a quick flashing of strong teeth, clenched as in a bite; his sense of humor draws blood. Whatever a Tuscan does, he does fully. There are no half measures, no shades of gray. Indifference is not part of the Tuscan's lexicon. And the Tuscan woman shares this "essential Tuscanity." Botticelli depicts her as the epitome of modesty: Naked or veiled, a Tuscan woman is a spiritual image of all that is pure. Boccaccio recognizes in her a bold carnality and brings her down to Earth. Dante identifies his Beatrice with divine grace, source of all inspirations. Piero della Francesca depicts her as a fully pregnant Madonna, the most divine womanly woman, heavenly and earthy, the essential mother. All of this is what a Tuscan woman is, and you will recognize her today: inspiration, partner, mother, and above all vital counterpart to the Tuscan man. "Behind every great man there is a great woman" does not apply in Tuscany: She shares equal billing and presence on the Tuscan stage. Here, Saint Catherine of Siena told the Pope what to do.

Anything Tuscan is essentially unique. Even at the table, this uniqueness reveals itself: The cuisine excels in genuine ingredients cooked simply. On an open-fire grill or in a pot, it is a direct, parsimonious cuisine, one that insists on substance and shuns complicated, elaborate concoctions. It favors dense, green olive oil and white cannellini beans and purple cabbage and all the other hearty produce of the land, flavored without ambiguity with rosemary, sage, bay leaf, garlic. Like most soups, theirs were born of humble origins as a one-dish meal. And yet, in their simplicity and their sophisticated frugality, they have a directness that makes them Tuscan—different from the others.

It is said that frugality is a strong Tuscan trait, a thrift edging on avarice. It is, again, a lie: No other people or country has given, with such incredible disproportion, so much, and so generously, to the rest of the world.

Bread Soup

Minestra di pane

We have been always puzzled by the soup's name, since bread is *not* the main ingredient, as they would make you believe. "They" are the many country places where the soup is offered, especially in the Chianti region.

Regardless, it is a good example of the many peasant soups cooked in the summer, using fresh vegetables from the garden. This may not always be easy in the twentieth-century American kitchen, so we have tried to list practical alternatives for today and have made pork rind, which adds a bit of gelatin to the soup, an optional ingredient.

2½ pounds fresh kidney beans, or 3 cups canned and drained (approximate)

2 slices salt pork

1 large onion

2 celery ribs, trimmed

3 garlic cloves

5 sprigs flat-leaf parsley, stems removed

4 fresh basil leaves

1 dried red pepper pod, seeded, or a dash of Tabasco

¼ cup (approximate) olive oil

½ cup dry red wine, such as Chianti

6 purple cabbage leaves, cut in thin strips

(Cont.)

Shell the fresh beans and place in a soup pot with 8 cups of salted water. Bring to a slow boil. Fresh beans cook in 15 to 20 minutes. Canned beans need only be heated through.

Mince together the salt pork, onion, celery, 2 of the garlic cloves, parsley, and basil. Sauté the mince and the red pepper pod with the olive oil over medium heat until golden. Raise the heat and add the wine, stirring until almost totally evaporated.

Boil the cabbage strips for 5 minutes. Drain well.

Peel and seed the plum tomatoes, chop coarsely, and add to the sauté pan with pepper to taste. Cook for about 15 minutes, then add the sauté mixture to the bean pot. Add the boiled, drained cabbage strips and the pork rind, if using. Cook at a low simmer for about 30 minutes.

Oven-toast the bread and rub the slices gently with the remaining garlic clove. Divide the toasts among the serving dishes, ladle the soup over them, and serve.

1½ *pounds (12 approximate)*
plum tomatoes, fresh or canned

Pepper

6 ounces blanched pork rind
(optional)

6 to 12 slices whole wheat bread,
oven-toasted

Potato Soup

Zuppa di patate

Cut the potatoes in relatively large pieces and place them in a big soup pot with water to cover. Mince the celery, onion, parsley, carrot, and basil, and add to the pot along with the tomatoes and the olive oil. Bring the pot to a boil, lower the heat, and cook for about 25 minutes, or until the vegetables are tender. Add salt and pepper to taste.

Pass the soup through a sieve into a second pot, and heat it well. Add warm water if the soup needs thinning, and add salt to taste.

Place the croutons in a soup tureen, add the soup, and serve.

2½ *pounds baking potatoes,*
peeled

6 cups water

1 large celery rib

1 medium onion

12 sprigs flat-leaf parsley, stems
removed

1 large carrot

4 to 5 leaves fresh basil

12 ounces canned plum tomatoes,
peeled and crushed

½ *cup virgin olive oil*

Salt

Pepper

2 cups croutons, fried or toasted

Cabbage Minestrone

Minestrone di cavolo

1 small head savoy cabbage

½ head common cabbage

4 medium potatoes

2 turnips

½ medium onion

½ medium carrot

1 celery rib, trimmed

5 sprigs flat-leaf parsley, stems
  removed

4 tablespoons olive oil

2 tablespoons unsalted butter

8 cups broth (beef, chicken, or
  mixed)

Salt

1 cup cooked white kidney beans
  (cannellini)

¾ cup small macaroni

Freshly ground pepper

Grated Parmesan cheese

Peel off any damaged bits of the savoy and common cabbages, remove the cores, and cut the remaining cabbage in thin strips. Cook in boiling water for 5 minutes, and drain well.

Wash and peel the potatoes and turnips, and cut in thin slices. Mince the onion, carrot, celery, and parsley.

In a soup pot, sauté the mince in the olive oil and butter over moderate heat until the onion is translucent and wilted. Add the cabbage strips, potatoes, and turnips, and stir well. Cook for 1 or 2 minutes, until the vegetables are well coated with the sauté. Add the broth, and bring the pot to a boil. Lower the heat and cook about 10 minutes, or until the potatoes and turnips are tender. Add salt to taste.

Add the cooked beans and the macaroni, and cook for 8 minutes, or until the pasta is tender. Serve immediately with freshly ground pepper and grated Parmesan cheese.

Tuscan Rice and Bean Soup

Minestra di riso e fagioli alla toscana

This soup has a number of versions, depending on the season, the town you are in, and who is at the stove. If you cannot find canned white kidney beans (cannellini), you may substitute dried navy (pea) beans or Great Northern beans, soaked overnight and then cooked.

In a soup pot, sauté the minced onion, parsley, and celery in the olive oil until nicely browned. Add the crushed tomatoes and cook for about 10 minutes.

Add the escarole, stir, and cook for 1 to 2 minutes.

Drain the beans, reserving and measuring their liquid. Add ½ of the beans, the rosemary, and bay leaf to the pot. Add enough water to the reserved liquid to measure 8 cups total. Add the salt and pepper to taste. Bring to a boil, and cook another 2 to 3 minutes.

Just prior to serving, return the pot to a boil, and add the rice. Stir and cook about 14 minutes, or until the rice is tender.

Crush the remaining ½ of the beans, and add them to the pot. Remove and discard the rosemary sprig and the bay leaf. Simmer for another 1 to 2 minutes.

If the soup is too thick for your taste, add a bit of very hot water.

Serve with freshly grated Parmesan cheese.

1 small onion, minced

4 to 5 sprigs flat-leaf parsley, minced with stems removed

1 celery rib

½ cup olive oil

1½ cups canned plum tomatoes, crushed

1 pound escarole, or ½ small cabbage, washed and chopped coarsely

2 cups canned white kidney beans, undrained

1 rosemary sprig

1 bay leaf

Salt

Freshly ground pepper

¾ cup short- or medium-grain rice

Freshly grated Parmesan cheese

Livorno's Bean and Cabbage Soup

Bordatino

The marriage of beans and cabbage in soups is a popular and happy one in almost all the regions of Italy. Tuscany alone has several variations on the same theme. What makes this *bordatino* different from the others is the addition of corn polenta as a thickener.

8 cups water

2 teaspoons salt

1½ to 2 pounds fresh kidney beans, unshelled

1 fresh rosemary sprig

1 onion, minced

1 carrot, minced

1 celery rib, minced

1 garlic clove, minced

10 sprigs flat-leaf parsley, minced with stems removed

6 tablespoons olive oil

3 tablespoons tomato paste

1 small red cabbage, cored and cut in thin strips

½ cup fine cornmeal (or instant polenta)

1 cup cold water

In a soup pot, bring the water and salt to a boil. Shell the beans and add with the rosemary to the boiling water. Lower the heat and cook until the beans are tender, about 20 minutes. Remove the rosemary sprig and discard.

Press the beans and cooking water through a sieve or food mill, forming a puree. Add enough warm water to make about 8 cups of liquid.

In a soup pot, sauté the minced onion, carrot, celery, garlic, and parsley in the olive oil over low heat, stirring and mashing until reduced to almost a paste. Add the tomato paste, stir, and simmer for 2 to 3 minutes, until well mixed. Stir in the cabbage strips and cook until wilted. Add the bean puree, and bring the soup to a boil.

Mix the cornmeal and cold water until smooth. Pour into the soup, stirring constantly with a wooden spoon. Cook about 30 minutes (much less if using instant polenta), until the cornmeal is cooked. Serve hot.

Note: By adding more cornmeal and increasing the cooking time, the soup may be so thick as to be cut with a knife; or it may be thinned by adding warm water. It is up to the cook to taste and decide on the final flavorings and consistency.

Bean and Cabbage "Reboiled" Soup

Ribollita

Anyone who has visited Florence in any season has been offered *ribollita.* It is part of the trend of reviving old peasant fare and making it, with reason, fashionable. Originally it was a *zuppa di fagioli alla fiorentina* (Florentine bean soup), and what was left over and reheated the day after became *ribollita* ("reboiled"). Today the soup is generally made to be served intentionally "reboiled" the next day.

This very thick and hearty soup is frequently served at room temperature, with a dribble of extra-virgin olive oil on the individual servings.

In a soup pot, sauté the onion, celery, and garlic in the olive oil until limp. Add the leeks, rosemary, and thyme. Dilute the tomato paste in the hot water, add to the sauté, and cook for 10 minutes.

Boil the cabbage for 3 or 4 minutes in about 2 quarts of salted water. Drain, reserving the cooking water.

Stir the cabbage into the soup pot and cook 3 to 4 minutes, until the cabbage is well flavored. Add the reserved water and simmer for 15 to 20 minutes.

Stir in the undrained beans, season with salt and pepper to taste, and cook until the beans are heated through.

Serve immediately, with toasted bread slices. Or let rest until totally cold, then bring to a boil again and serve warm or at room temperature, topped with a dribble of extra-virgin olive oil.

1 small onion, minced

1 celery rib, minced

2 garlic cloves, minced

½ cup olive oil

2 leeks, white part only, sliced

3 to 4 sprigs rosemary

3 to 4 sprigs thyme

½ cup tomato paste

1 cup hot water

1 small purple cabbage, cored and sliced fine

2 cups canned white kidney beans, undrained

Salt

Freshly ground pepper

6 to 12 slices Italian-style white bread, oven-toasted

Extra-virgin olive oil

Grosseto's Mushroom and Egg "Cooked Water" Soup

Acquacotta

"Cooked water" appears, with local variations, on the table of many different regions, describing a soup made with humble ingredients. This one is made with wild porcini mushrooms, abundant for the picking in the Grosseto woods. To be true to the spirit of the soup, in this country—fresh porcini being rare and expensive—we resort to more affordable farm-grown mushrooms, flavored with imported dried porcini.

½ ounce dried porcini mushrooms

1 cup warm water

1¼ pounds fresh mushrooms, preferably portabella

4 tablespoons olive oil

2 garlic cloves

1½ teaspoons plus a dash of salt

Pepper

10 ounces fresh plum tomatoes, peeled and crushed

8 cups hot water

2 tablespoons unsalted butter

3 tablespoons all-purpose flour

4 tablespoons grated Parmesan cheese

12 small slices Italian-style white bread, oven-toasted

4 egg yolks (see Note)

Soak the porcini mushrooms in 1 cup of warm water for 15 to 20 minutes. Drain the mushrooms, reserving the soaking water, and squeeze them dry, making sure they are free of sand. Chop the mushrooms coarsely.

Clean the fresh mushrooms carefully, and cut them in thin slices.

In a soup pot sauté the olive oil and garlic over moderate heat until golden. Remove and discard the garlic.

Add the fresh mushrooms, the chopped porcini, and a dash of salt and pepper. Cook over low heat until the mushrooms begin to wilt, then add the reserved soaking water, making sure that it is free of sediments.

Add the crushed tomatoes, stir, bring to a boil, and cook for 1 to 2 minutes, until the mushrooms are well flavored and the sauce has reduced a bit. Add the hot water and the salt, and simmer for 10 to 15 minutes.

Melt the butter in a small saucepan. Add the flour and stir with a wooden spoon until it resembles a smooth paste. Cook over medium heat, stirring constantly, to obtain a lightly colored roux. Remove from heat and stir in the Parmesan cheese.

Stir the roux into the soup, mixing it well. Let simmer for 1 minute. Divide the toasts among the serving dishes, ladle the soup over the toasts, and serve.

Note: For a variation, break the egg yolks into a soup tureen, add the Parmesan, and beat with a whisk. Pour the boiling hot soup over the eggs, stir well, and serve over the toasts.

Egg and Marsala Soup

Cinestrata

Cinestrata is a light soup somewhat reminiscent of zabaglione, served in soup cups as a light opener for a formal dinner.

Place the egg yolks in a bowl and whisk well. Slowly stir in the marsala and the broth. Whisk well and add the cinnamon.

Pour the mixture into a soup pot over low heat, and bring to a very low boil. Cut the butter into small pieces and add to the pot. Cook and stir until the soup begins to thicken evenly. Remove from heat and pour the soup into warmed soup cups. Sprinkle with the sugar and nutmeg and serve immediately.

6 egg yolks

¾ cup dry marsala wine

6 cups cold chicken broth

½ teaspoon cinnamon

4 tablespoons unsalted butter

½ teaspoon sugar

½ teaspoon freshly grated nutmeg

Tomato Soup, Peasant Style

Pappa al pomodoro

In culinary terms, *pappa* means a puree or, in ordinary parlance, a light soup suitable for the very young and the very old. This *pappa al pomodoro* is a much beloved tomato soup—the inspiration for children's books and songs.

In Tuscany, this soup is frequently prepared in larger batches because, as they say also for many other soups, it is even better when warmed over. It is also served decorated with small basil leaves floating on the surface.

1 pound (approximate) dried-out Italian bread

6 cups canned peeled plum tomatoes, undrained

2 tablespoons olive oil

6 cups chicken broth

6 garlic cloves

10 fresh basil leaves, chopped

Salt

Freshly ground pepper

Extra-virgin olive oil

Heat oven to 300°F.

Remove and discard any hard crusts of the bread, and then cut the bread in small cubes.

Pass the tomatoes through the fine disc of a food mill into a soup pot. Add 2 tablespoons olive oil, the chicken broth, and the bread. Skewer the garlic cloves with toothpicks for easy retrieval, and add with the basil to the soup pot.

Bring to a low boil and add salt and freshly ground pepper to taste. Lower the heat and let the soup simmer for 20 to 30 minutes, or until all the bread has dissolved (you may help the process by mashing the cubes with a wooden spoon), and it has the consistency and smoothness of a tomato puree or heavy cream.

Retrieve and discard the garlic, and serve the soup either warm or at room temperature, garnished with a dribble of extra-virgin olive oil.

Ricotta Green Dumplings in Broth

Gnocchi verdi di ricotta in brodo

Cook the frozen spinach in boiling water for 5 minutes. Drain well. When cool, squeeze the spinach to remove as much water as possible.

Put the ricotta in a bowl, add the spinach, and mix well. Add the egg, nutmeg, and salt, and stir. Add 4 tablespoons of the Parmesan cheese and ½ cup of the flour, and mix well.

Put the remaining flour on a plate and flour your hands.

Scoop up a teaspoon of the mixture and roll it with the palms of your hands until you have a dumpling about the size of a bing cherry or a small walnut. Roll the dumpling on the plate to coat with the flour. (Depending on the moisture content of the ricotta or of the spinach, you could need more dry ingredients. To test, drop one or two of the first dumplings in boiling broth to see if they keep their shape. If so, continue making dumplings until all the mixture is finished. If not, add a little more cheese or flour.)

As you roll the dumplings, line them up on a well-floured cookie sheet. (Do not stack them, as they might stick together, and you would have to start all over again.)

Bring the broth to a boil and add the dumplings a few at a time. As they are cooked and rise to the top, scoop them out and divide them among warmed soup dishes.

When all the dumplings are cooked, ladle the hot broth over the gnocchi and serve with the remaining 4 table-spoons of Parmesan cheese.

1 ten-ounce package frozen chopped spinach

1 pound ricotta

1 egg

½ teaspoon freshly grated nutmeg, plus more as needed for garnish

1 teaspoon salt

8 tablespoons grated Parmesan cheese

¾ cup flour

7 cups broth (beef, chicken, or mixed)

Tuscan Fish Soup

Cacciucco

Choose as many different kinds of fish as your market has to offer. The use of red wine makes the *cacciucco* a particularly Tuscan specialty from Livorno.

FOR THE FISH:

3 small squid

½ pound medium shrimp

1 small sea bass

1 whole red snapper

½ halibut steak

2 small fish, such as gray mullet, porgy, or rosefish

Cooked meat of 1 lobster (5 ounces approximate)

FOR THE SOUP:

4 garlic cloves

1 dried cayenne pepper pod, seeded

⅓ cup olive oil

3 to 4 sprigs flat-leaf parsley, minced with stems removed

1 carrot, peeled and minced

1 celery rib, minced

1 small onion, minced

After you have cleaned the squid and the shrimp (reserving the shells), clean the fish as needed: Cut off and reserve the heads of the sea bass, red snapper, and halibut, and cut the bodies in chunks. Clean the smaller fish but leave whole, heads and all.

In a large soup pot, sauté 3 of the garlic cloves and pepper pod in the olive oil until the garlic is golden and the pepper dark brown. Remove the garlic and pepper and discard.

Add the minced parsley, carrot, celery, and onion, and sauté until limp and the onion is translucent. Add the wine, and when it is almost completely evaporated, add the tomatoes, and salt. Bring the pot to a boil, lower the heat, and let the sauce simmer for about 10 minutes.

Add the reserved shrimp shells, fish heads, the small whole fish, and the hot water to the pot. Return to a boil, lower the heat, and cook for about 20 minutes, or until the small fish have nearly disintegrated.

Remove from the heat, and stir with a wooden spoon, mashing the fish. Press the whole mixture through a sieve, squeezing from it as much juice as possible, into a large stovetop casserole. Bring the puree to a boil, add the squid, the shrimp, and the chunks of sea bass, red snapper, and halibut. By now the soup should be rather thick and just barely cover the fish. If not, add a bit more boiling water to cover.

Lower the heat and simmer for 5 minutes, or until the big chunks of fish flake when touched with the tines of a fork. Be careful not to overcook. Cut the cooked lobster meat into bite-size pieces and add to the soup.

Rub the toasted bread slices with the remaining 1 garlic clove and place a slice in each warmed soup dish. Equally distribute the fish and shellfish over the toasts, and ladle in the soup. Serve immediately.

1 cup dry red wine

2 cups canned, peeled plum tomatoes, crushed

1 teaspoon salt

2 cups hot water, or more as needed

6 slices Italian-style bread, oven-toasted

Umbria

Dandelion "Cooked Water" Soup
Acquacotta all'umbra

Onion Soup
Cipollata

Tagliolini Soup
Tagliolini in brodo

Chickpea and Noodle Soup
Minestra di ceci con quadrucci

Winter Wheat Soup
Minestra di farro

Omelet Soup with Anchovies
Minestra di frittata all'umbra

Meat Soup in the Style of Perugia
Minestra di carne alla perugina

Umbria

The much-used slogan for this region is "Italy has a green heart: Umbria." Anatomically, if Italy had a pumping heart, Umbria is where you would expect it to be. And green the region is, seemingly at all seasons. Anchored solidly in the east to the Central Apennines, it moves down in an alternating series of hills and plains, crossing the large central Tiber Valley, to end in the west with the river Paglia at the Lazio border.

Umbria is one of the smallest Italian regions and one of the five without a seashore. Nonetheless, it is rich in the sweet, clear water of rivers, in mineral and thermal springs, and in lakes, among them Lake Trasimeno, the largest in Italy outside the big northern lakes. Umbria has a gentle, familiar geography: We recognize it in the idealized landscapes of Renaissance painters. It even seems to have, as in the paintings, perennial white billowing good-weather clouds to enliven and give depth to its skies.

The region is divided into only two provinces, Perugia and Terni, cities so different from each other that they could be on two different continents. Perugia, which is also the region's capital, retains its elegantly intellectual, mystic medieval character; from high up it overlooks the splendid Tiber valley and its flanking hills. Terni lies flat in the basin of the Nera River, the power source for the town's factories. It is a major, no-nonsense industrial town dedicated to iron and steelworks. However, both cities are a stone's throw from the many gemlike towns that enrich Umbria. And these, given the size of the region, rub elbows with each other: Terni is eighteen miles from Spoleto, of the Festival of Two Worlds fame, the same distance as Spoleto is from Foligno and Foligno from Assisi, Saint Francis's town. From there to Perugia is only ten miles, and from there to Gubbio, the towered town at the east border with the Marche, is but twenty-five miles. . . . And so is Todi, and then Chiusi, bordering with Tuscany, and then lofty

Orvieto in the west, rubbernecking over Lazio. The hopscotch can go on and on from one town to another, and it will cover, artistically and historically, all of the Middle Ages, the golden era of Umbria.

Etruscans and Romans set the foundations for the construction that was to follow, leaving substantial traces of their civilizations' passage. Umbria was an essential stop in the European cultural Grand Tour of the 1700s and 1800s: Goethe, Montaigne, Ruskin, Montesquieu, Stendhal—poets, intellectuals, artists all combed Umbria for learning and inspiration. But, undoubtedly, an indelible medieval imprint to the whole region was left by Saint Francis, patron saint of Italy. There is hardly a hamlet in all of Umbria where his mystic presence is not felt, culminating in the apotheosis that is Assisi and its basilica. The humble, diminutive saint who called the Moon and Water sisters, Earth and Fire brothers, talked with birds and beasts, and embraced poverty as a serene way of life, gave Catholicism a human measure and pace. With his band of ragtag happy friars, simple poets, and artists, he preached and was able to show the strength of faith, as opposed to the pomp and temporal power of Papal Rome. Perhaps Saint Francis's vision of a simple, unencumbered life is part of the makeup of the local character, or perhaps his teachings have been well absorbed by the Umbrians, because that is the mood of the people and of the country one feels today, traveling the land. Missing are the loud theatricality, the ample gesturing, the flashy colors that are supposed to be an Italian's heritage; present are a calm, serene simplicity, a quiet, wry sense of humor, and a spontaneous generosity, the ability to unite the sacred and the profane, heaven and earth, in a simple dimension.

This whimsical approach to life can be seen in the shapes, colors, and designs of Umbrian artisans' work, as expressed in the copper and wrought-iron implements and the classic Deruta pottery. Mythical flora and fauna intricately chase each other in pastel shades of blue-green and light brick-browns, but the objects are very practical plates, goblets, and wine vessels: The imaginary monsters and flowers carry very real food and wine.

The local gastronomy echoes the character of the region and has been defined as being of "solid simplicity," not offering great flights of fancy. It takes advantage of the quality ("quantity" is a seldom-used word in Umbria) of the Perugian beef, of the sheep and goats raised in the valleys' green pastures, their cheeses, the furry and feathery game of its woods, and above all, the lean, acorn-fed pigs. It is all cooked simply, as if following monastic rules, and yet with a touch of refined elegance. A basic onion soup in Umbria becomes a *cipollata,* a delicate, creamy soup in which the onion's strong attributes are soaked away and only its sweetness and texture remain. But, to reinforce the contradictory values of everything Umbrian, to the simple cookery the region brings the most aristocratic, most expensive of ingredients: the truffle. And in winter, its glory season, Umbrians use the black, tuberous gem with abandon. In the little town of Norcia, nestled high in the Sibillini Mountains, they make an art of hog butchering. The Norcini have been known for centuries as real virtuosos of all manner of pork products, from salami to prosciutto: as a result, *Norcini* is synonymous with "pork butcher" and *Norcineria* has come to mean any store dealing in pork specialties.

That is one side; on the other, humble Norcia is the birthplace of Saint Benedict. As founder of the Benedictine Order in A.D. 529 he gave a new start to Western culture after the fall of the Roman empire.

Umbria: the sacred and the profane—all without boasting, but with a knowing smile.

Dandelion "Cooked Water" Soup

Acquacotta all'umbra

This *acquacotta* is said to be the one that inspired all the other regional versions: It was the soup of poor friars, who made it with donated old bread, wild dandelion greens (*cicoria*), herbs found in the fields, and water.

¼ cup olive oil

1 garlic clove, minced

1 onion

2 celery ribs, chopped

6 to 7 basil leaves

Sprig of fresh marjoram, or a
  pinch of dried oregano

4 to 5 plum tomatoes, peeled and
  chopped

2 pounds dandelion greens, well
  washed and coarsely chopped

8 cups warm water

2 teaspoons salt

6 to 12 slices dried-out Italian-
  style bread

4 eggs

2 to 3 tablespoons milk or water

In a soup pot, heat the olive oil and sauté the garlic, onion, celery, basil, and marjoram until the onion is limp and translucent. Add the tomatoes and cook for 5 minutes, to a sauce consistency. Stir in the dandelion greens and cook 5 minutes or until wilted, then add the water and salt. Bring to a low boil and cook for 15 to 20 minutes.

Put the dried-out bread slices in the bottom of the serving dishes.

Beat the eggs and mix well with the milk. Add a pinch of salt, and pour the mixture over the bread slices, allowing them to soak up the mixture. Ladle the boiling hot soup over all, and serve.

Note: Spinach may be substituted for dandelion greens. The beaten eggs may be stirred directly into the soup at the end of cooking.

Onion Soup

Cipollata

This soup requires soaking the sliced onions overnight in cold water to take away the strong odor and sharpness of common onions. It makes for a delicate and creamy onion soup—the soaking time is well spent.

Soak onion slices overnight (or for at least 6 hours) in abundant water in a pot with a tight-fitting lid. Drain thoroughly.

In a soup pot over medium heat, cook the minced salt pork and the olive oil until the pork has rendered its fat but is not crisp.

Add the onions to the pot. Increase the heat, stir, and add the basil. Cover the pot, lower the heat to simmer, and continue cooking for about 10 minutes, or until the onion slivers have wilted. Remove the cover but continue cooking until the liquid in the pot has almost totally evaporated.

Put the undrained canned tomatoes through a food mill, and add the puree to the onions.

Add the hot water, the salt and pepper to taste, and mix well. Cover the pot and simmer for 20 minutes.

Remove from heat. Beat the egg yolks, and stir them into the hot soup. While stirring, sprinkle in the Parmesan cheese, 1 tablespoon at a time. Serve hot over the toasted bread.

2½ pounds onions, peeled, cored, and very thinly sliced

3 ounces salt pork, minced

4 tablespoons olive oil

6 basil leaves, cut in thin strips

20 ounces canned peeled plum tomatoes, or 2 cups tomato-vegetable juice (V8 or similar)

4 cups hot water

2 teaspoons salt

Freshly ground pepper

3 egg yolks

6 tablespoons grated Parmesan cheese

6 to 12 slices Italian-style bread, oven-toasted

Tagliolini Soup

Tagliolini in brodo

A winter visit to the elegant Umbrian city of Perugia will produce, among others, the memory of *tagliolini in brodo*. It is a non-taxing dish, but essential are a superb beef broth and the freshest of homemade pasta.

1 batch four-egg homemade pasta (pages 256–260) cut in ⅛-inch wide, 8-inch-long tagliolini (very thin fettuccine), or 8 ounces fresh commercial pasta

8 cups beef broth

Freshly grated Parmigiano Reggiano cheese

Cook the freshly made pasta in the boiling broth for 2 minutes. Serve with the best grated cheese.

Chickpea and Noodle Soup

Minestra di ceci con quadrucci

Puree 2 cups of the undrained chickpeas. In a soup pot, combine the puree, the remaining 2 cups undrained chickpeas, and the broth, and bring to a boil. Smash the garlic cloves with the flat side of a knife. In a saucepan, sauté the garlic cloves, bay leaf, and rosemary in the olive oil until the garlic is golden brown, then allow to cool. Strain the olive oil through a sieve and add the oil to the chickpeas. Add the tomatoes and the quadrucci, and cook at a low boil until the pasta is done, 5 to 6 minutes.

Add salt and pepper to taste. The soup may be served at room temperature, topped with a dribble of extra-virgin olive oil.

3 to 4 cups canned chickpeas, undrained

7 cups chicken broth (or lightly salted water)

3 garlic cloves

1 bay leaf

2 sprigs fresh rosemary

4 tablespoons olive oil

2 to 3 plum tomatoes, peeled and coarsely chopped

2 cups quadrucci (⅜-inch pasta squares) or coarsely broken egg noodles

Salt

Freshly ground pepper

Extra-virgin olive oil

Winter Wheat Soup

Minestra di farro

It is said that sacks full of *farro,* hardy winter wheat, were carried as the main food staple by Roman soldiers as they headed out for conquest. Like many other simple country dishes, *farro* has enjoyed a sort of fashionable renaissance. The grain is not easily found on market shelves, but bulgur—cracked whole wheat—may replace it as a good substitute for *farro*'s texture and nutty taste. It is a sturdy soup to keep in mind when you have a ham bone on hand—or if you are out for conquest.

2 tablespoons olive oil

1 garlic clove

1 onion, diced

2 carrots, peeled and diced

2 celery ribs, diced

1 potato, diced

4 plum tomatoes, peeled and crushed

9 cups water

2 teaspoons salt

1 ham bone with a bit of meat left on it (or hog knuckle, see Note)

¼ cup fine-ground bulgur

1 tablespoon minced parsley

Freshly grated pecorino Romano cheese

In a soup pot, sauté in the olive oil the garlic and onion. When the onion is limp, add the carrots, celery, and potato, and cook for 5 minutes. Stir in the crushed tomatoes and cook for another 5 minutes. Add the water, salt, and the ham bone, bring to a boil, and simmer for 30 minutes. If necessary, depending on the quality of the ham bone, skim the surface of the soup.

Retrieve the bone, cut off any available bits of meat, and add them to the soup.

Return the soup to a boil, slowly stir in the bulgur, and cook, stirring occasionally, about 20 minutes, or until the bulgur is tender.

Serve hot, garnished with a sprinkling of minced parsley and pecorino Romano cheese to taste.

Note: The ham bone can be replaced by smoked hog knuckle, which will add a pleasant smoky flavor to the soup. But, before using it, boil it for 30 minutes, drain, and rinse.

Omelet Soup with Anchovies

Minestra di frittata all'umbra

This *minestra* combines the texture and the savory taste of a frittata with the smooth and soothing qualities of chicken broth. It is easily adapted to a varying number of portions, using 1 egg and 1½ cups of broth per serving.

In a bowl, mash the anchovy filets and mix with the parsley. Add a generous sprinkling of pepper. Add the eggs and beat thoroughly.

Cut each tomato in 8 wedges. Remove and discard the seeds and juice, and cut the wedges in small cubes. Combine the cubed tomatoes with the egg mixture. Add salt to taste.

Grease an omelet pan with a veil of olive oil. Heat the pan and pour in the egg mixture. Depending on the number of eggs and the pan size, make one or more omelets. When brown on the underside, turn the omelet: Let the omelet slide into a plate slightly larger than the pan; oil the pan again, then put the pan upside down on top of the plate and turn the two together, right side up. When the omelet is ready, set aside and allow to cool.

Cut the omelet into 1-inch strips, and cut the strips into squares. Distribute equally on serving dishes, pour the hot broth over them, and serve.

6 anchovy filets

6 teaspoons minced parsley

Freshly ground pepper

6 eggs

3 plum tomatoes, peeled

Salt

Olive oil, as needed

7 to 8 cups hot chicken broth

Meat Soup in the Style of Perugia

Minestra di carne alla perugina

1 pound twice-ground lean beef

2 eggs

3 tablespoons Parmesan cheese, plus more as needed

½ teaspoon salt

½ teaspoon ground white pepper

All-purpose white flour, as needed

2 carrots, minced

2 leeks, white part only, minced

2 celery ribs, minced

¼ cup olive oil

7 cups hot beef broth

Put the ground beef in a bowl, and add 1 whole egg and 1 egg yolk (reserve the remaining egg white), the Parmesan cheese, the salt, and the white pepper. Mix thoroughly, and form cherry-sized meatballs (the smaller the better). Dust them lightly in flour and set aside.

In a soup pot, sauté the carrots, leeks, and celery in the olive oil until the vegetables are limp. Stir into it the reserved egg white, and add the broth slowly. Mix, bring to a low boil, and cook 15 to 20 minutes, or until the broth is reduced to about 6 cups.

Add the meatballs and simmer for 5 to 10 minutes, depending on the size of the meatballs.

Serve warm with a sprinkle of Parmesan cheese.

Le Marche

Asparagus and Rice Soup
Minestra con punte di asparagi

Fresh Bean Soup
Zuppa di fagioli freschi

Pea Soup, Macerata Style
Pisellata alla maceratese

"Raggedy" Egg Soup
Stracciatella marchigiana

Cornmeal Dumpling Soup
Minestra di frascarelli

Chickpea and Short-Rib Soup
Minestra di ceci e spuntature

Adriatic Fish Soup
Brodetto d'Ancona

Pesaro's Mussel Soup
Muscioli alla pesarese

Le Marche

The early morning mist lifting up from the valleys reveals rivers and green hills, well-ordered farms, orchards and vineyards, a landscape dotted with hilltop crenelated castles and walled-in towns. It is like a curtain rising on a play: Le Marche, Italy. (The pronunciation stresses a hard *k:* "Mar-kae," not the English, The Marches.)

It is a little-known play, especially abroad. The Marchigiani are self-effacing, more interested in diligent work and the cheerful appreciation of the best life has to offer than in self-promotion. They will tell you that their region is somewhat overshadowed by its more flashy neighbors, Tuscany and Umbria. And yet with its history, art, architecture, natural beauty, gastronomy, and religious mysticism, it offers at least as much as, if not more than, the more glamorous and traveled places of Italy. All of these riches, a couple of hours' drive from Rome or Florence, come in a relatively small package: From north to south Le Marche is about one hundred miles long. West to east, its mountain valleys descend from the high peaks of the Central Apennines and, like fingers reaching for the sea, touch the Adriatic in about fifty miles.

To the traveler the region appears rich, relaxed, and tidy, even in the nature of its geography: Chains of hills follow one another, soothingly drawing the eye ever farther. The banks of rivers and streams are lined by oaks and poplars; it is a gentle landscape, but here and there the land offers a surprise—like the snaking of a white road that cracks the landscape, or an isolated old tower that adds an exclamation point to the panorama—that gives to it the charm and color of a Renaissance landscape painting.

Travel in Le Marche should be like *assaggini,* "sample tastes," in which a small portion of a particular dish is savored, unhurriedly, before going on to the next offering.

Wandering around Le Marche, following the beckoning of one turreted town after another, is like weaving in and out of the early Middle Ages and the Renaissance. Each place has something unique to offer—a local poet described the land as "a nest of saints and of tyrants, of poets and painters, of heroes and ruffians." But finally Urbino, its province's biggest magnet, will pull you in.

Urbino's massive Palazzo Ducale at first appears to dominate the cityscape. Brainchild of Federico da Montefeltro, enlightened prince and *condottiere* of the fifteenth century, the enormous yet elegant construction was described as "a city in the shape of a palace." Urbino, along with Florence, Siena, Arezzo, and a few other enlightened places, was at the core of the Renaissance's birth. Raphael, one of its most illustrious sons, was born in Urbino, and so was Bramante, the architect of the Rome of the popes; many of the big names in the fields of science, history, letters, and jurisprudence revolved around the Renaissance fulcrum that was Urbino.

In a concentrated way, Urbino sets the tone for the rest of Le Marche. A fast thirty miles from Urbino is Pesaro, on the Adriatic coast, and there one can find a jewel—be it a portal, a palace, a square, or a villa—reminiscent of each century, from pre-Roman times to today. Among Pesaro's prides, and undoubtedly the most immediately recognized around the world, is Gioacchino Rossini, master of the comic opera and of joyful music. The strains of *Barbiere di Siviglia, L'Italiana in Algeri, Semiramide,* and *La Gazza Ladra,* created by the good-natured, happy, and rubicund Rossini, seem to fill Pesaro's air. Rossini was also known, at home and abroad, as a *buona forchetta*—a good fork. It would not be too far-fetched to speculate that he had a particular appreciation for his Pesaro's classic fish soup *brodetto,* the basic requirement of which is thirteen—no more, no less—different varieties of fish and shellfish, cooked ever so slowly in a fish broth.

Ancona, the region's capital and the largest city of Le Marche, with a population of around 100,000, offers large avenues, elegant buildings and shops, a state university, and a very active economy. The town was founded by the Greeks, prospered under the Romans, became an independent seafaring republic—strong enough to challenge the Republic of Venice—and then fell under the control of the popes and was the last holdover of the Papal States until 1860, when it joined the Kingdom of Italy.

An extra-good reason to stop in Ancona is to explore the authentic regional cuisine of its immediate surroundings. As we were compiling a list of foods and wines to taste and places to go, the name of Jesi, a walled hilltop city, came up on top for its dry white wine, Verdicchio.

Once produced in small quantities of variable quality, Verdicchio is today a consistently good wine: Many small farmers have joined in cooperatives, and Verdicchio appears on the honor roll of Italian wines. A well-known wine expert describes the best Verdicchio as "pale straw in color, with greenish tints. It has a taut dryness and a good fruit-acid balance. It leaves a lingering taste of bitter almonds on the palate. . . ."

In a small hamlet we found a simple sign over a door inviting us to stop: WINE AND FOOD. The establishment is a simple square room; the light from its only window falls on a group of old men playing cards. The light sparkles on the glasses on the table: It looks as if Caravaggio had just passed by and arranged the tableau. A middle-aged lady, ruddy and rotund, drying her hands on her apron, approaches us from the kitchen. At our wish for a bite to eat, she suggests that we will have to do with "what's in the house." We approve, she smiles, and in a moment she is back with a terra-cotta pitcher of chilled wine and a bowl of thick soup. "Peasant fare," she says as an apology. With our consent, she pours a thin thread of olive oil on the soup. The oil catches the light and sparkles green-gold. It is the kind of food to be savored slowly, with eyes closed, as in meditation.

The wine that pours from the pitcher is clear and cool. We would not have been surprised if told that the lady had stomped the grapes herself. It is pale straw in color, with greenish tints. It even leaves a lingering taste of bitter almonds. . . . It is Verdicchio, no doubt about it. And here, it is fantastic—the best.

To complete the discovery of Le Marche, one cannot ignore the last two provinces and their capital cities: Macerata and Ascoli Piceno.

Macerata is a large town, and it reflects Le Marche's marriage of art and history, of commerce and culture. Ruins prove its Roman origin, but the town bloomed with the Renaissance, of which today it is a perfectly preserved showcase.

Similar in spirit is Ascoli Piceno, a town that respects the past and adds to it as history rolls on. "It is a city that you can visit in a day, but that you will never forget," our guide to Ascoli tells us. It is unique, he says, an adjective confirmed by the city's Piazza del Popolo, the historic center and heart of the city. The square is crowded and alive at any hour of the day with people of different classes, professions, and ages who meet here to discuss politics, sports, food, or fashion. The human patchwork is stitched together by children, who run around chasing pigeons and each other.

The two cities' gastronomy is also particular: there they will tell you *si mangia bene,* "one eats well." Good food is a matter of fact, not an exception.

And it is a fact favored by the nature of the region: The woods of the mountains supply all the aromatic herbs for the stuffing and flavoring of the famous *porchetta* (whole baby pig on a spit), as well as the wood pigeons and wild mushrooms that are made for each other. The green hills, moistened by sea breezes, supply all the garden and orchard produce; the olive trees donate the great olives that appear pickled, preserved, fried, and stuffed. From the coastal plains come the free-range fowl (none other is accepted) that most of the time—and like everything else—will end up stuffed. Pig, pigeon, quail, chicken, fish, and vegetables will stuff one another in what seems to be password and prerogative of Le Marche's gastronomy.

One step to the south from Ascoli Piceno and you are in Abruzzo; one to the west and you are in Lazio; either way you have run out of Marche and a difficult chore is in front of you: To choose, among all of the sampled *assaggini,* real or metaphorical, which to return to and have more. As for ourselves, we know: We are going back for seconds of everything.

Asparagus and Rice Soup

Minestra con punte di asparagi

This is a soup for those who grow their own asparagus or have access to the first of the crop—the short, slender, small asparagus, the tips of which are quick-cooking and very tender.

1 pound fresh early asparagus

1 onion, minced

2 tablespoons unsalted butter

2 tablespoons tomato paste

1 cup hot water

6 to 7 cups hot beef broth

1 cup short- or medium-grain rice

Salt

Freshly ground pepper

Grated Parmesan cheese

Cut the tips (about 1½-inch lengths) from the asparagus, and rinse and drain well. (Save the remaining stems for another use.)

In a saucepan, sauté the onion in the butter and cook until the onion is limp and nicely browned. Stir the tomato paste into the hot water, and add the mixture to the onion. Bring to a boil, add the asparagus tips, cover, and simmer until the asparagus is tender.

In a soup pot, bring the broth to a boil and add the rice. When the rice is almost cooked (about 12 minutes), add the asparagus-tomato sauce. Cook another few minutes until the rice is tender. Add salt and pepper to taste. Let rest a minute or two and serve the soup with the Parmesan cheese.

Fresh Bean Soup

Zuppa di fagioli freschi

Fresh is the operative word for this soup. Red or white, the fresher the beans, the better.

Shell the beans and put them in 12 cups boiling salted water to cook (about 20 minutes). When cooked, drain the beans and reserve 6 cups of the cooking water.

Combine the minced parsley, celery, and salt pork, until almost a paste.

In a soup pot, sauté the mince in the olive oil with the pepper pods for 2 to 3 minutes. Add the wine, and cook until it evaporates. Dilute the tomato paste in the hot water and stir into the soup pot. Cook for 2 to 3 minutes, then add the cooked beans, the reserved 6 cups water, and a dash of pepper. Cover and simmer for 15 minutes.

Add salt to taste. Serve with the toasted slices of bread.

3 pounds fresh red or white beans, unshelled

1½ teaspoons salt

5 to 6 tablespoons minced flat-leaf parsley

2 celery ribs, minced

3 ounces salt pork (or pancetta, if available), minced

⅓ cup olive oil

1 to 2 hot red pepper pods (or Tabasco sauce to taste)

¼ cup dry red wine

3 tablespoons tomato paste

1 cup hot water

Freshly grated pepper

6 to 12 slices Italian-style bread, dribbled with olive oil and oven-toasted

Pea Soup, Macerata Style

Pisellata alla maceratese

*3½ ounces lean salt pork,
    chopped coarsely*

1 small onion, minced

1 garlic clove, minced

*1 cup (loosely packed) flat-leaf
    parsley, minced*

*4 to 5 leaves fresh marjoram,
    minced*

2 tablespoons olive oil

*2 cups fresh plum tomatoes,
    peeled, seeded, and chopped
    coarsely*

8 cups water

2 teaspoons salt

Dash of freshly ground pepper

*20 to 24 ounces frozen baby peas
    (or 1½ pounds fresh shelled
    peas)*

2 tablespoons very fine cornmeal

*6 to 12 (depending on size) slices
    Italian-style bread, oven-
    toasted*

In a soup pot, sauté the salt pork, onion, garlic, parsley, and marjoram in the olive oil.

Add the tomatoes and the water to the pot. Add salt and pepper, and bring to a boil. Add the peas, lower the heat, and simmer for about 20 minutes, or until the peas are cooked to your taste. Slowly sprinkle in the cornmeal, stir well, and cook another 3 to 4 minutes.

Serve the soup with the toast. No cheese.

"Raggedy" Egg Soup

Stracciatella marchigiana

Stracciatella literally means "torn to rags," because when the egg mixture is dropped into boiling broth, it cooks into shredded threads. There are many regional versions, all delightful. By eliminating the lemon zest and bread crumbs, and adding ¼ teaspoon freshly grated nutmeg and ¼ teaspoon ground white pepper, you can make another version, *Stracciatella alla romana.*

In a soup pot, bring the broth to a boil.

Break the eggs into a bowl and beat them well. Add the grated lemon zest and the salt. Continue beating and add the Parmesan cheese, bread crumbs, and flour. This should result in a rather liquid, well-blended mixture.

Pour the egg mixture into the boiling broth in a steady stream, stirring as you pour. Let the soup boil briefly and serve.

8 cups beef or chicken broth (or a mixture of the two)

4 eggs

Zest of 1 lemon, grated

½ teaspoon salt

4 tablespoons grated Parmesan cheese

2 tablespoons bread crumbs

1 teaspoon flour

Cornmeal Dumpling Soup

Minestra di frascarelli

2 eggs

2 tablespoons unsalted butter,
    melted

½ teaspoon salt

¼ teaspoon white pepper

¼ teaspoon freshly grated nutmeg

¾ to 1 cup fine cornmeal

8 cups water, lightly salted

6 to 7 cups vegetable broth

Grated Parmesan cheese

Place the eggs and melted butter in a bowl and beat well with a whisk, adding salt, pepper, and nutmeg as desired.

Slowly sprinkle the cornmeal into the bowl, stirring it into the egg mixture with a wooden spoon. Keep adding and stirring until you have a smooth paste, of cookie dough consistency. Let rest for 30 minutes.

Bring the water to a boil, and lower the heat slightly. Using two teaspoons, scoop the cornmeal mixture out of the bowl with one spoon and scrape it into the hot water with the other. Let the *frascarelli* (dumplings) simmer about 8 to 10 minutes, until cooked and solidified.

While the dumplings cook, bring the broth to a boil in a soup pot. With a slotted spoon, scoop out the *frascarelli* and divide among six serving dishes. Pour the hot broth over them, and serve topped with a generous sprinkling of grated Parmesan cheese.

Chickpea and Short-Rib Soup

Minestra di ceci e spuntature

In a soup pot, sauté the minced parsley, onion, and garlic in the olive oil and butter over medium heat until onion is limp and golden.

Add the short ribs and brown them quickly in the mince. Stir in the wine, allow to evaporate, and add the crushed tomatoes.

Add the chopped celery and arugula to the soup pot, and add salt and pepper to taste. Stir and cook at a low boil for 4 to 5 minutes to slightly thicken the sauce.

Add the undrained chickpeas and the hot water. Cook uncovered at low boil for 30 minutes, or until the soup has boiled down and thickened a bit. The short-rib meat should fall off the bones.

Serve with the toasted bread and top with the pecorino Romano cheese.

4 to 5 sprigs of flat-leaf parsley, minced with stems removed

1 small onion, minced

1 garlic clove, minced

4 tablespoons olive oil

2 tablespoons unsalted butter

2 pounds short ribs of pork, cut in 2-inch lengths

¼ cup dry red wine

2 cups plum tomatoes, peeled and crushed

1 celery rib, chopped

5 to 6 arugula leaves, chopped

Salt

Pepper

20 ounces canned chickpeas, undrained

8 cups hot water

6 to 12 slices of Italian-style bread (whole wheat if possible), oven-toasted

Grated pecorino Romano cheese

Adriatic Fish Soup

Brodetto d'Ancona

Aside from Ancona, almost every fishing village in Le Marche claims *brodetto* as its own. Fixed points of a traditional *brodetto* are that it should be made with thirteen different kinds of fish—with the essential inclusion of skate wing—and flavored with vinegar.

FOR THE FISH:

3 small squid, cleaned (page 248)

½ pound large shrimp, peeled and deveined

1 pound small cherrystone clams

½ pound skate wing, cleaned

4 pounds mixed fish (whiting, mullet, haddock, halibut, flounder, porgy, or scup), cleaned, scaled, and cut in chunks

FOR THE SOUP:

1 large onion, thinly sliced

1 garlic clove

½ cup olive oil

½ cup wine vinegar

2 cups canned peeled plum tomatoes

(Cont.)

In a soup pot over medium heat, sauté the onion slices, garlic, and olive oil. When the garlic is golden, discard it. When the onion slices become translucent, add the squid and cook and stir about 1 minute, or until the tentacles open up and turn to pink-and-purple in color. Remove and reserve the squid.

Add the vinegar and cook until it has evaporated.

Add the tomatoes, mixed fish, clams, skate, and shrimp.

Add just enough water to cover the fish. Bring the pot to a boil, reduce the heat, and cook until the clams have opened and the thickest pieces of fish flake easily when touched by a fork, 10 to 15 minutes. Discard any clams that remain closed. Add salt and pepper to taste.

Warm the bread in a hot oven. Divide the *brodetto* among the soup dishes, sprinkle with the chopped parsley, and serve with slices of hot bread.

1 tablespoon salt

Freshly ground pepper

6 to 12 slices Italian-style bread

5 sprigs flat-leaf parsley, chopped with stems removed

Pesaro's Mussel Soup

Muscioli alla pesarese

Debarb and scrub the mussels clean. Soak in cold water for 30 minutes, changing the water a few times. Probe and squeeze the mussels; throw away the ones that will not close tightly.

Heat the oil in a large saucepan or pot. Drain the mussels and add to the pan with the parsley, basil, lemon juice, and a generous dash of pepper. Stir, cover tightly, and let cook over high heat for 5 to 6 minutes, or until the mussels open.

Scoop out the mussels and place them in a large serving bowl. Strain the remaining liquid through a sieve lined with cheesecloth, and ladle the "mussel broth" into individual soup dishes. Warm the bread in a hot oven.

Note: The idea is for each individual to fetch a mussel from the bowl, scoop some of the broth with the half shell containing the mussel, and use it as a spoon. The soup should be accompanied by oven-hot bread and cellar-cold Verdicchio wine.

4 pounds (approximate) very fresh mussels

¼ cup olive oil

1 cup (loosely packed) flat-leaf parsley, minced with stems removed

1 cup (loosely packed) fresh basil leaves

Juice of 2 lemons

Freshly ground pepper

Fresh Italian-style bread

Lazio

Easter Soup
Brodetto pasquale

Viterbo's Summer Vegetable Soup
Minestra alla viterbese

Rice and Fresh Fava Bean Soup
Minestra di riso e fava fresca

Pasta and Cauliflower in Skate-Wing Broth
Pasta e broccoli in brodo d'arzilla

Pasta, Bean, and Potato Soup
Pasta e fagioli freschi

Pasta and Chickpea Soup, Roman Style
Pasta e ceci alla romana

Egg Pasta Squares and Pea Soup
Quadrucci e piselli

Islanders' Lentil Soup
Zuppa di lenticchie all'isolana

Anzio's Mussel Soup
Zuppa di cozze all'anziate

Fish Soup, Roman Style
Zuppa di pesce alla romana

Lazio

Lazio: It all started here. From a small clan of shepherds, with Rome at its core, Latium became the mighty Roman Empire, the forge of Western civilization, the giver of laws, the known world. As in a biblical parabola, in a few more centuries Latium returned to where it began: at the beginning of the 1800s shepherds led their flocks at pasture among the ruins of the temples and the forums. *Sic transit gloria mundi.*

There was an attempt in the mid-1930s to bring Rome back to the prestige of the Empire. But history had run out of its supply of Caesars, and Mussolini failed.

Yet, if the power of Rome is gone, its beauty has remained, and never can one savor it so fully as on a fall day. The air is crisp, transparent, and everything has the clean lines and sharp edges of an etching. Colors are brilliant and come in a thousand hues; even the shadows glow with light. If that day happens of a Sunday, then it is unsurpassable. The city is quiet, people smile and move without hurry, willing to share all this immense wealth: the beautiful city, the limpid air, the cloudless blue sky. These are the kinds of days when Rome, more than ever, puts a spell on you. One feels privileged to be in Rome, Roman if even for a moment, able to drink it all in, and thirsty for more. The perfect cup for the heady elixir is the Pincio Terrace, on top of one of the seven hills, in the Villa Borghese. From that vantage point, all Rome is there in front of you, its cupolas and towers and monuments; the huge dome of Saint Peter's Basilica dents the horizon and dominates all. On a fall Sunday, lean on the Pincio's marble balustrade and wait: At the stroke of twelve, from the Gianicolo hill all the way across town, the old "noon cannon" will boom, and in a moment, as if at a starter's gun, all the churches' bells will let loose, calling and answering each other. It is a joyful noise that once heard will rarely be forgotten. Thousands of pigeons and starlings give body to the sound, circling the air, rising and diving and rising again with the pealing of the bells: Their sound bounced by the seven hills, here are the bells of Santa Maria Maggiore, and there of Saint John in Lateran, and then of Saint Paul Outside the Walls, and of hundreds of other churches and chapels and basilicas, but above them all of *Er Campanone*, the Big Bell. It is said that only a Roman, wherever and forever, will recognize the deep, sonorous, majestic voice of Saint Peter's great bell: It makes the sky vibrate so that it will reach not only his ears but his heart.

Besides Rome, Lazio has four other provincial towns. They are mostly agricultural centers, which defines the character of the whole region. Its total western border is lapped by the Tyrrhenian Sea; Civitavecchia is the only commercial port, significant mostly for its traffic with Sardinia. Other minor fishing ports are at Fiumicino and Anzio which, with a few even smaller ones, supply enough fish to give Lazio a seafood gastronomy larger than one would suspect.

Almost totally ignored—abroad as much as in Italy itself—is the presence in the region's waters of a small cluster of islands. Ponza is the largest of the five of the Pontine archipelago, part of the string of volcanic jewels that begins with the uninhabited island of Palmarola in the north and ends with the islands of Ischia and Capri in the south.

The Pontine Islands are connected with the continent by frequent *aliscafi,* hydrofoils and ferryboats that join the port of Anzio with the blue-green harbor of Ponza. White and pink houses perched around and above the half-moon bay look like spectators in a Greek amphitheater; ancient shows are acted out daily by the fishermen who land the catch of the night, lining the dock with rows of shining, metal-black swordfish.

As seen from its highest point, Ponza resembles a lizard basking in the sun, head pointing south. It is about five miles long and measures a little more than a mile at its widest point. Every inch of usable land is terraced to the edge of precipitous cliffs; left and right the long body is scalloped by harbors and bays carved away by sea and wind, their waters the color of crystal-clear tropical seas.

From Roman times to a more recent era, the island was used not as a resort but primarily as a place of exile. Emperor Augustus started the trend with his Lex Julia, a law that prescribed exile for adultery. Julia Augusta, his own daughter, was the first exiled to the island, a gilded cage, because he deemed her "not too thrifty with her honor." With time, the interpretation of the law became more flexible and was used mostly to put opponents out of the way, a custom revived centuries later by the Fascists, who shipped political undesirables out to Ponza.

Now that the exile image has disappeared, people are appreciating the archipelago for what it is: quiet islands of fishing villages, with an incredibly mild and constant climate, with ever-changing, bewildering seascapes—an accessible, affordable family paradise.

The islands' coasts are pierced by many sea caves of rare beauty, but the most interesting among them is the cave of Pontius Pilate, so named because legend says that Pilate was born in Ponza (hence Pontius). The cave is of interest because it was a moray eel breeding fishery. The

Romans, inordinately fond of the eels, created a system of breeding pools in the cave and in adjacent manmade grottoes. As the eels grew, they were moved from one pool to the next, and when they reached the last, it was time for the pot. It is said that since the vicious morays were as gluttonous for Romans as Romans were for them, some masters sent unruly slaves "to feed the eels"—in the most literal way.

Moray eel is still a delicacy, and for good reason: Its delicious milk-white, firm flesh is very close to that of lobster. But the island's real specialties are from the earth: *cicerchie,* halfway between small chickpeas and beans; and the local tiny, dark, and flavorful lentils which, for the unique qualities of Ponza's soil, have an intense earthy flavor. A Ponza lentil soup is to the people of Ponza what the *campanone* is to a Roman: Something you do not forget.

The cuisine of Lazio resists pigeonholing. "Imagination is what the food lacks" is how a known food expert describes the cuisine of Lazio. Another writer, taking Rome as representative for the whole region, says: "A cuisine made rich by the glorified use of poor ingredients, produced to satisfy the people's urge to make a feast of any event, pagan or religious, and celebrate around a groaning table. . . ." And then—and we agree—"the region lays one of the most pungently tasty and vividly colored tables in Italy."

Easter Soup

Brodetto pasquale

The accent in this broth is fresh marjoram, the aroma of which, legend has it, represents the happiness of spring. To be true to Roman tradition, the broth should be made with spring lamb, also a symbol of spring and of Easter.

---

7 cups chicken broth

6 egg yolks

Juice of 1 small lemon

6 to 12 slices Italian-style white bread, oven-toasted

Grated Parmesan cheese

12 fresh marjoram leaves, chopped (or ½ teaspoon dried marjoram)

In a soup pot, warm the broth but do not allow it to boil.

In a second soup pot, beat the egg yolks with a whisk and add the lemon juice and then the warmed broth.

Continue to work slowly with the whisk, and place the pot over medium heat for 5 minutes, or until the broth takes on a creamy texture.

Distribute the toasts evenly in the serving dishes, and garnish with the Parmesan cheese and the marjoram. Pour the soup over the toasts and serve.

Viterbo's Summer Vegetable Soup

Minestra alla viterbese

With a grater, grate the potato and the carrot into a pulp.

In a soup pot combine the grated potato and carrot, the sliced zucchini and onion, the minced garlic, celery, parsley, and basil, and the tomatoes. Add the water and salt, and bring to a boil. Reduce the heat and simmer for 15 minutes.

To avoid lumps, dilute the flour in 1 cup cold water, then pour it slowly into the soup, stirring constantly, and cook for another 10 to 15 minutes.

Remove from the heat, and stir in the butter. When the butter has melted, add the cheese. Serve immediately.

1 potato, peeled

2 carrots, peeled

1 zucchini, sliced in thin rounds

1 onion, sliced thin

1 garlic clove, minced

1 celery rib, minced

12 sprigs flat-leaf parsley, minced with stems removed

6 to 7 fresh basil leaves, minced

2 ripe tomatoes, peeled and chopped

7 cups water

2 teaspoons salt

½ cup semolina flour

1 cup cold water

4 tablespoons unsalted butter

4 tablespoons grated Parmesan cheese

Rice and Fresh Fava Bean Soup

Minestra di riso e fava fresca

3 ounces lean salt pork, minced

1 large onion, minced

2 tablespoons olive oil

3 pounds fresh fava beans, unshelled

2 tablespoons tomato paste

9 cups hot water

¼ cup medium-grain rice

3 tablespoons butter

1½ teaspoons salt, plus more as needed

In a soup pot over high heat, sauté the minced salt pork and onion in the olive oil until the onion bits are limp.

Shell the fresh fava beans, add them to the pot, and sauté briefly. Dilute the tomato paste in 1 cup of the hot water, and add to the soup pot. Lower the heat and cook 5 to 10 minutes, depending on the size of the fava beans.

Stir in the rice and add the butter. While stirring, add the remaining 8 cups hot water and the salt. Cook another 12 to 14 minutes, or until the rice is tender. Serve hot.

Pasta and Cauliflower in Skate-Wing Broth

Pasta e broccoli in brodo d'arzilla

This ancient soup is from Testaccio, once a poor section of Rome. The soup used "poor" ingredients—Roman broccoli and skate—to come up with a very tasty soup. Roman broccoli is purple-tipped cauliflower; the *arzilla*—skate—should be very fresh.

Put the skate wing pieces in a pan adequate to the size. Add the cold water, salt, garlic, onion, the celery ribs, and the carrot.

Place the pan over medium heat, and bring to a boil. Reduce the heat and simmer for 25 to 30 minutes, or until the fish falls apart. Strain; press and squeeze the skate and its broth through a fine sieve into another pan or bowl, and reserve.

In a soup pot over medium high heat, sauté the minced garlic, parsley, and anchovies in the olive oil and Tabasco until the mince begins to brown. Add the chopped tomatoes and the white wine to the soup pot and cook at a low boil for 10 minutes. Stir in the reserved skate broth, and bring the soup pot to a boil. Reduce the heat, cover, and simmer 15 minutes.

Break the cauliflower into flowerets, cutting the largest in half and the edible part of the stems in pieces.

Add the cauliflower to the soup pot and continue cooking at a low boil until the cauliflower pieces are almost tender. Add the pasta, and increase the heat to return the pot to a boil. Once boiling, stir, lower the heat, and simmer for 8 minutes, or until pasta is tender. Serve immediately.

FOR THE SKATE BROTH:

3 pounds skate wing, cleaned

8 cups cold water

1½ teaspoons salt

2 garlic cloves

1 onion

2 celery ribs

1 small carrot

FOR THE SOUP:

2 garlic cloves, minced

6 sprigs flat-leaf parsley, minced with stems removed

2 anchovies, minced

⅓ cup olive oil

2 to 3 dashes Tabasco

8 canned plum tomatoes, chopped

½ cup dry white wine

(Cont.)

1 purple cauliflower (1½ pounds, approximate)

2 cups small macaroni (tubettini, ditalini, or spaghetti broken in 1- to 2-inch pieces)

Pasta, Bean, and Potato Soup

Pasta e fagioli freschi

3½ ounces pork rind

1 pound fresh white kidney beans (cannellini), unshelled

6 cups cold water

2 teaspoons salt

¼ pound prosciutto, minced

1 medium onion, minced

4 tablespoons olive oil

2 cups canned plum tomatoes, drained and chopped

1 celery rib, chopped fine

1 potato, peeled and cubed

Dash of freshly ground pepper

10 ounces fettuccine, in 2-inch lengths

In a small saucepan, place the pork rind in boiling water for 10 minutes, then drain. Cut the rind in ½-inch strips.

Shell the beans and put them in a pot with the cold water, salt, and the pork rind strips. Bring to a boil, reduce the heat, and simmer until the beans are almost tender, about 20 to 30 minutes.

In a saucepan, sauté the minced prosciutto and onion in the olive oil. Add the tomatoes, celery, potato, and the pepper. Stir over high heat for 1 to 2 minutes, then add the vegetable mixture to the soup pot with the beans.

Simmer for 10 minutes, or until the potatoes are tender. Add the fettuccine and continue cooking, stirring occasionally, until the pasta is tender. The soup should be reasonably thick; add some warm water if necessary. Let rest a few minutes before serving warm. (It can also be served at room temperature.)

Pasta and Chickpea Soup, Roman Style

Pasta e ceci alla romana

This is a much-beloved Roman soup, a favorite in the old Trastevere district of the city. Traditionally the pasta used was the *rimanenze,* the remainders of the various bins of pasta—long and short mixed together—that merchants would sell cheaply. It was a good way of using remainders and also gave the soup an interesting, different texture.

In a large soup pot, sauté the minced salt pork in the olive oil over medium heat until translucent.

Add the garlic, tomatoes, rosemary, and 2 cups of the chickpeas. Mash the remaining 1 cup chickpeas and add to the soup pot. Add the hot water, bring to a gentle boil, and simmer for 10 minutes.

Increase the heat and add salt to taste. When the pot has come to a good boil, add the pasta.

Reduce the heat and cook, stirring occasionally, until the pasta is tender, about 12 to 14 minutes. Fish out and discard the garlic cloves. Serve hot or at room temperature, garnished with a sprinkling of Romano cheese.

4 ounces lean salt pork, minced

½ cup olive oil

4 garlic cloves

2 to 3 plum tomatoes, peeled and chopped coarsely

1 sprig fresh rosemary, or 2 tablespoons dried

3 cups canned chickpeas, drained and rinsed

7 cups hot water

Salt

8 ounces penne, mostaccioli, or elbow macaroni

Grated pecorino Romano cheese

Egg Pasta Squares and Pea Soup

Quadrucci e piselli

Quadrucci are homemade fettuccine, cut into small squares. They are available commercially, but if you want to make your own, you can wrap dried commercial fettuccine or egg noodles in a clean dishtowel and break with your hands.

3 tablespoons unsalted butter

1 celery rib, minced

½ carrot, peeled and minced

1 onion, peeled and minced

3 ounces lean salt pork, minced

1 pound shelled fresh peas, or 10-ounce package frozen baby peas

7 cups hot chicken broth

1 batch two-egg pasta (see pages 256–258) cut as fettuccine and then in squares, or 6 ounces commercial egg pasta (fettuccine or egg noodles, broken in small square pieces)

Grated Parmesan cheese

In a soup pot over medium heat, melt the butter, add the minced celery, carrot, onion, and salt pork and sauté until the mince is golden and limp. If using fresh peas, add them now and cook for 2 to 3 minutes. Add the hot broth (and if using them, the frozen peas), bring to a boil, and cook for 8 minutes. Add the pasta and continue boiling until the pasta is tender, about 5 minutes.

Stir the soup and sprinkle in the Parmesan cheese so that it melts without lumping. Cook 1 minute more and serve.

Islanders' Lentil Soup

Zuppa di lenticchie all'isolana

Wash the lentils in cold water and drain well.

In a soup pot over medium heat, sauté the garlic cloves in the olive oil until golden. Remove the cloves and discard. Add the chopped onion, celery, and parsley and sauté until golden-green and wilted, about 10 minutes. Stir in the wine, and cook until almost evaporated.

Dilute the tomato paste in ½ cup of the warm water, and add to the pot. Cook another 5 minutes, or until mixture resembles a thin sauce.

Add the lentils, the remaining 8 cups warm water, the bay leaf, and salt. Bring the pot to a boil, reduce the heat, and boil gently for 15 minutes.

Add the celery to the lentils and continue to slow boil for 15 minutes, or until lentils and celery pieces are tender.

In the meantime, in a frying pan brown the sausages (if using), pricking them frequently to let them release as much fat as possible. Drain them, allow to cool a bit, and then slice in ½-inch rounds. Add the sausage to the lentils. Add salt to taste. Serve hot.

2½ cups dried lentils

3 garlic cloves

4 tablespoons olive oil

1 medium onion, chopped

4 stalks celery with leaves, cut in ½-inch pieces

6 parsley sprigs

½ cup dry red wine

3 tablespoons tomato paste

8½ cups warm water

1 bay leaf

2½ teaspoons salt

2 Italian-style sausages, sweet or hot (optional)

Note: On the island of Ponza, the lentil soup would be enriched not with sausages but with eel, grilled in sausage-length pieces and then added to the soup.

Anzio's Mussel Soup

Zuppa di cozze all'anziate

The difference between this and other mussel soups is the presence of the celery, which gives it a truly different taste and texture.

4 to 4½ pounds mussels

2 garlic cloves

2 large dried cayenne pepper pods, seeded, or ½ teaspoon powdered hot red pepper

6 tablespoons olive oil

4 celery ribs, sliced thin

¾ cup dry white wine

2 cups canned peeled plum tomatoes, chopped

3 tablespoons minced fresh flat-leaf parsley

1 loaf Italian-style bread

Scrub the mussels clean, debarb them, and rinse well.

In a soup pot, sauté the garlic and hot pepper in the olive oil until the garlic is golden. Discard the garlic and pepper pod, if you wish. Stir in the celery slices and sauté for 2 to 3 minutes, then add the wine. Cook 1 to 2 minutes, and add the tomatoes. Cook for 4 minutes, increase the heat, and add the mussels. Cover the pot, and cook for 5 minutes, or until the shells have opened.

Add the parsley, stir, and serve in warmed soup plates with hot Italian-style bread to dip in the soup.

Fish Soup, Roman Style

Zuppa di pesce alla romana

Eating a Roman fish soup transcends the gastronomic experience. It becomes almost a mythical affair, an enthusiastic communion with the riches of the sea.

Fish heads, bones, shells, and all end up on the plate—and only fingers can do justice to what is served. It is a somewhat messy operation, especially for the uninitiated, but it is more than worth the experience. Naturally, the soup may be made by cooking the bones and the edible parts separately, but then it will be, even if very good, just another fish soup.

Clean and scale the fish, but save the heads and tails and, if the larger fish is fileted, the bones. Cut the fish into bite-size chunks.

Clean the squid (see page 248); scrub, debarb, and wash the mussels thoroughly. Peel the shrimp, and reserve the shells.

In a saucepan over medium heat sauté the garlic cloves and pepper pods in the olive oil until the garlic is golden and the pepper a deep brown. Add the minced onion and celery, and sauté for 1 minute. Add the fish heads, tails, bones, and shrimp shells. Increase the heat and cook, stirring, for 3 to 4 minutes. Add the wine and cook until it almost evaporates. Remove from the heat. Pass the saucepan contents through a sieve, pressing and squeezing the solids, and letting the juice drain into a soup pot.

Bring the contents of the soup pot to a boil and add the tomatoes and the salt. Boil, stirring, for 2 to 3 minutes; add the squid and cook until it turns pink and lavender in color, about 2 minutes. Add the mussels, stir well, and

FOR THE FISH:

1 whiting

1 small red snapper or rose fish

½ halibut filet

1 porgy, scup, or tautog

½ pound small squid

½ pound mussels

½ pound medium shrimp

FOR THE SOUP:

2 garlic cloves

2 dried cayenne pepper pods, seeded

½ cup olive oil

1 small onion

1 celery rib

(Cont.)

1½ cups dry white wine

3 cups canned peeled plum tomatoes, chopped

2 to 3 teaspoons salt

1 loaf Italian-style bread

cover the pot. When the mussels have opened, in 3 to 5 minutes, scoop them out with a slotted spoon and set aside.

Add the fish to the pot, beginning with the thickest. If needed, add enough warm water to barely cover the fish. Cover the pot and continue cooking about 5 minutes, or until the fish begins to flake. Return the mussels to the pot until heated through.

Divide the shrimp, mussels, squid, and fish chunks among the serving dishes, and ladle the soup over the fish.

Serve with hot, crusty, Italian-style bread—if you really want to be Roman, dunk it in the soup.

Abruzzo e Molise

Abruzzi Lentil and Chestnut Soup
Zuppa di lenticchie all'abruzzese

Dandelion Greens Soup
Cicoriella, cacio e ova

Thin Spaghetti in Fish Broth
Spaghettini in brodo di pesce

Crepes in Broth
Scrippelle 'mbusse

Broth and Bacon Bits
Brodosini

Artichoke, Chicken Liver, and Meatball Soup
Minestra di carciofi e polpettine

Ortona's Fish Soup
Zuppa di pesce d'Ortona

Abruzzo e Molise

The visitor who thought Italy had exhausted its allotted share of mountains with the arc of the Alps should come to Abruzzi—and reconsider. Here, at the geographical center of Italy, mountains are a constant, imposing presence. At 9,500 feet, the Gran Sasso d'Italia is the highest peak of the Apennines, followed closely by the Maiella massif, the Velino and the Sirente, the Laga and the Morrone Mountains, and, to underline it all with a surprise, the perennial glacier of Calderone.

Entering the region from the north, the west, or the south is an uphill journey: The horizon is blocked by mountains, the roads must share space with torrents and riverbeds or squeeze through gorges and passes. The approach from the east should be easier: Abruzzo e Molise's eastern border is 85 miles of smooth, sandy beach lapped by the Adriatic, interrupted in a few spots by rocky cliffs.

Since prehistory, the natural conditions helped the various local tribes to repel external influences and also, given the hardy geography and climate, to shape the inhabitants' strong, tenacious, loyal, and feisty character. Largely a population of shepherds, forced to pass through other tribes' turf during the seasonal migrations of the herds, they developed a strong warlike nature, assisted by a quick-reflex intelligence—traits that convinced the ancient Romans to keep these neighboring mountain people as allies. These elements have been distilled into today's Abruzzesi: square-shouldered, stubborn, and cunning mountain people.

The mountainous complex contains an incredible geographical variety, with highlands and plateaus, valleys and bowl-like water basins, hills rolling sharply to the sea, a variety of undeniable beauty. There is a continuity of customs and traditions in the Abruzzi. Pagan rituals, shielded from outside influences more than in other regions of Italy, have resisted Christianity. Many churches and abbeys have their foundations on old pagan temples, and many a religious cere-mony shows a pagan origin. Pan and Ceres have been replaced by saints as protectors of harvests: Saint Anthony Abbot assures a good slaughtering of pigs, Saint Blaise protects against sore throats.

Throughout the historical vicissitudes of prehistory, of the middle ages, and of the Renais-sance, towns and cities such as the capital L'Aquila, Teramo, Chieti, Pescara, Sulmona, and scores of family-owned villages developed and accumulated a wealth of artistic and architectural trea-sures. With the unification of Italy, the political, religious, and economic climate changed quite drastically. The region's long-standing isolation was broken, and with easier transit within and outside the area, Abruzzi has been brought abreast of the rest of the nation. Today, its culture, folklore, and arts, its numerous and valuable crafts, its gastronomy, and its natural beauty are val-ued to their full extent; Rome, only a short drive away, has made of Abruzzo e Molise a play-ground, for its skiing in the winter and its seashores in the summer. Visitors to the many reservations and parks may enjoy the wild flora, from the velvety alpine edelweiss to cerulean-blue and saffron crocus, from primeval pine and beech to maple forests; numerous wild faunae make their home there—wolf and antelope, wild mountain goat, deer, bear, and soaring royal eagle.

And in all seasons, it is not uncommon to come to Abruzzi just to partake of its savory and fra-grant cuisine. It is for the tasty palette of local ingredients and for the inspired, sometimes whim-sical, way of using them that Abruzzo e Molise is a veritable nursery of famous chefs, a father-to-son heritage.

Cornerstones of the cuisine are the ubiquitous hot red pepper *peperoncino* (here affectionately named *diavolillo,* or "little devil"); the locally grown saffron, as good as Spain's; the sheep and goat cheeses; the many pork products of lean mountain pigs; and the pasta made from Molise's hard winter wheat, renowned the world over. Above all, the local cuisine and its cooks seem inspired by a controlled balance of colors, tastes, and textures. And yet in an economy derived from a restrained, parsimonious handling of all goods, a culinary tradition is the *panarda,* a meal in which the host must offer no fewer than *thirty* courses. And the guests, having accepted, *must* finish them all, at risk of great offense to the host. It must be a tradition left over from Roman times: *una tantum, licet insanire*—once in while, it's good to let go and be wild!

Abruzzi Lentil and Chestnut Soup

Zuppa di lenticchie all'abruzzese

This is a late fall/winter soup, for the time when new chestnuts reach market. On a chilly night, when roasting chestnuts in the fireplace, roast a few more and save them for this soup.

Soak the lentils in enough cold water to cover for approximately 2 hours prior to cooking.

Drain the lentils and place them in a soup pot with 8 cups of water, the salt, and the bay leaf. Cover the pot and bring to a boil. Reduce the heat and simmer until the lentils are tender, about 30 minutes.

Cut salt pork and chestnuts in small pieces. In a saucepan over medium heat, sauté the salt pork, chestnuts, thyme, basil, and marjoram in the olive oil until the salt pork bits are lightly browned. Add the wine, stir, and cook until the wine evaporates.

Dilute the tomato paste in the ½ cup hot water, and add it to the pan along with pepper to taste.

Add the contents of the saucepan to the cooked lentils. Stir and simmer for another 10 minutes. It is a reasonably thick soup, but if needed, thin it with a little warm water.

In the meantime, dribble the bread slices with a little olive oil and toast in a hot oven.

Place the bread slices in the bottoms of the serving dishes, ladle the soup over the toasts, and serve immediately.

1½ cups lentils

8 cups water

1 teaspoon salt

1 bay leaf

3 ounces salt pork

15 to 20 chestnuts, roasted and peeled

2 to 3 thyme leaves

2 to 3 basil leaves

2 to 3 marjoram leaves

3 tablespoons olive oil

½ cup dry red wine

1 tablespoon tomato paste

½ cup hot water

Pepper

6 to 12 slices Italian-style bread

Olive oil

Dandelion Greens Soup

Cicoriella, cacio e ova

The "revitalizing" of the blood at every change of season was one of our many family rules for good health and clean living. This cleansing was achieved by various home remedies: Considered excellent for spring was the consumption of *cicoriella,* wild dandelion greens picked as soon as they appeared among the weeds of the fields.

1 cup water

1 teaspoon salt

1½ pounds dandelion greens, trimmed and washed

2 carrots, peeled

1 onion

2 celery ribs, trimmed

1 bunch (4 ounces) flat-leaf parsley

3 ounces lean salt pork

3 tablespoons olive oil

7 to 8 cups beef broth

2 eggs

6 tablespoons grated pecorino Romano cheese

In a large pot bring the water and salt to boil. Add the washed greens with only the water that clings to the leaves. Cover the pan, reduce the heat, and cook about 15 minutes, or until the stems of the dandelion greens are tender.

Drain the greens in a colander, rinse with cold water, and squeeze from the greens as much moisture as possible. Chop the greens finely.

Mince together the carrots, onion, celery, parsley, and salt pork. In a soup pot sauté the mince in the olive oil until it is lightly brown. Add the sautéed mince to the chopped greens. Cook, stirring, for 2 to 3 minutes. Add the broth.

Beat the eggs with 2 tablespoons of the cheese. Add to the greens and stir well.

Slowly bring the mixture to a boil. As soon as the soup bubbles up, remove from the heat. Serve with the additional grated cheese.

Thin Spaghetti in Fish Broth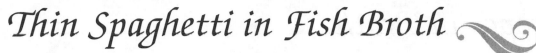

Spaghettini in brodo di pesce

In a wide-bottom pan, sauté the garlic, anchovies, and pepper pods in the olive oil until the garlic is golden and the anchovies nearly dissolved.

Add the celery, carrot, and bay leaf. Cook and stir 1 to 2 minutes, then add the tomatoes and salt to taste. Cook at a low boil for 15 minutes, then allow to cool. Pass the mixture through a sieve, collecting the tomato sauce in a soup pot.

Add the fish broth, stir well, and return to a boil.

Break the spaghettini with your hands into 2-inch lengths, and add to the boiling broth. Cook for 6 to 7 minutes, or until the pasta is tender.

Serve garnished with a sprinkle of minced parsley.

3 garlic cloves

6 anchovy filets, mashed

1 to 2 dried red pepper pods

½ cup olive oil

1 celery rib, chopped coarsely

1 carrot, peeled and chopped coarsely

1 bay leaf

1½ pounds plum tomatoes, peeled and crushed

Salt

1½ quarts fish broth (see page 255)

10 ounces spaghettini

3 to 4 tablespoons minced flat-leaf parsley

Crepes in Broth

Scrippelle 'mbusse

Scrippelle is the dialectal version of the Italian *crespelle,* which in turn is the version of the French *crepes;* 'mbusse is Abruzzese for "in broth." Whatever the linguistic derivations, this is a delightful and classic regional soup.

4 to 5 tablespoons grated
    Parmesan cheese

4 to 5 tablespoons grated
    pecorino Romano cheese

4 eggs

¼ teaspoon salt

⅛ teaspoon freshly grated nutmeg

2 tablespoons milk

1 tablespoon flour

3 to 4 tablespoons minced flat-
    leaf parsley

Unsalted butter, as needed

6 to 7 cups chicken broth

Combine the Parmesan and Romano cheeses.

In a small bowl, beat the eggs well and add the salt, nutmeg, and milk. When thoroughly beaten, sprinkle in the flour, the parsley, and 2 tablespoons of the cheese mixture. Dilute the eggs if necessary with 1 to 2 tablespoons cold water to turn it into a thin batter, the consistency of heavy cream.

With the butter, barely grease a well-seasoned 8-inch omelet pan. Place the pan over medium heat and spoon in just enough of the egg mixture to cover the bottom of the pan, forming a thin crepe. Cook until golden, then turn carefully and cook the second side. Set the crepe aside on a plate.

Continue making crepes until all the mixture is used. Divide the cheese mixture for the number of crepes and sprinkle on each evenly, then roll each up on itself and set aside.

While the *scrippelle* are being made, bring the broth to a boil. Evenly divide the *scrippelle* among the serving dishes. Pour the hot broth over them. Serve with more mixed grated cheese, if desired.

Broth and Bacon Bits

Brodosini

Roll the fresh pasta dough just slightly thicker than for fettuccine. Cut it by hand into ½-inch-wide strips, and then into 1½- to 2-inch lengths.

In a saucepan, sauté the minced salt pork and the red pepper pod, if using, in the olive oil until the bits are either crisp or only barely translucent.

In a soup pot, bring the broth to a boil. Add the pasta and the sautéed pork bits, and cook the pasta until done, about 4 to 5 minutes.

Serve warm.

1 batch three-egg homemade pasta (pages 256–260)

4 ounces lean salt pork or bacon, minced

2 tablespoons olive oil

1 dried red pepper pod (optional)

8 cups beef broth

Artichoke, Chicken Liver, and Meatball Soup

Minestra di carciofi e polpettine

Cardoons, like artichokes, belong to the thistle family. The Abruzzi region is famous for producing especially white tender cardoons in the late fall, and its cardoon soup is renowned. Substituting the more readily available artichokes makes for a nonseasonal soup that is quicker to prepare.

FOR THE SOUP:

1 ten-ounce package frozen artichoke hearts

Juice of 1 lemon

3 large egg yolks

1 cup grated Parmesan cheese

4 chicken livers, cleaned and cut in pieces

2 sage leaves, crumbled

1 tablespoon unsalted butter

8 cups hot chicken broth

FOR THE MEATBALLS:

10 ounces ground veal or twice-ground lean beef

2 eggs

½ cup grated Parmesan cheese

Plunge the artichoke hearts into lightly salted boiling water and simmer for 4 minutes. Drain well.

Place the artichokes in a bowl with the lemon juice; coat well and set aside.

For the meatballs: Mix the ground veal with the 2 whole eggs, the ½ cup Parmesan cheese, and the parsley. If needed, add bread crumbs until the mixture is firm enough to be shaped into balls about the size of a bing cherry. Let the meatballs rest.

In a small pan, sauté the chicken livers and sage leaves in the butter until lightly browned. Set aside.

In a soup pot, bring two quarts of lightly salted water to a boil. Drop in the meatballs, and cook for 3 to 4 minutes. Scoop them out and drain well.

Beat the egg yolks with the Parmesan cheese.

Scoop the artichoke hearts out of the bowl and cut them in quarters.

In a second soup pot, combine the artichokes, chicken livers, and meatballs. Add the egg mixture and stir carefully with a wooden spoon to coat. Pour the hot chicken broth slowly into the meat mixture. Bring to a low boil over medium heat. Stir carefully, and cook for 1 minute. Serve.

2 tablespoons minced parsley

1½ cups (approximate) dried, unflavored bread crumbs

Ortona's Fish Soup

Zuppa di pesce d'Ortona

Roast the bell peppers over a flame or under a broiler, turning so that all sides are charred and blistered. Peel the charred skin under running water, then core and cut the peppers in ½-inch strips.

In a shallow pan (large enough to hold all the fish in one layer), sauté the pepper pods in the olive oil until the pods are dark brown. Discard the pods and let the oil cool a moment before adding the tomatoes. Increase the heat until the tomatoes start to bubble. Mash the tomatoes with a wooden spoon; reduce the heat and simmer for 10 minutes, or until the tomatoes have blended with the oil and the liquid has reduced a bit.

Add the roasted pepper strips and the oregano (and the powdered red pepper, if using). Bring the mixture to a boil, and add the wine. Cover the pot, reduce the heat, and cook for 10 minutes.

Meanwhile, clean the sea bass and snapper, reserving the heads and tails. Cut each fish body in 3 to 4 chunks and

FOR THE SOUP:

2 sweet bell peppers, green or red

4 tablespoons olive oil

2 dried red pepper pods, seeded, or ½ teaspoon powdered cayenne pepper (see page 246)

2 cups canned peeled plum tomatoes, chopped

½ teaspoon dried oregano

½ teaspoon salt

1 cup dry white wine

1 packet (0.005 ounce) Abruzzese saffron

¼ cup hot water

2 tablespoons minced parsley

6 slices Italian-style bread, oven-toasted

FOR THE FISH:

1 sea bass or black bass (¾ to 1 pound, approximate)

1 red snapper (¾ to 1 pound, approximate)

¾ pound squid, cleaned and cut in rings (page 248)

½ pound shrimp

½ pound halibut steak

2 pounds mussels

Salt

set aside. (The fish should not be filleted; do so if you wish, but reserve the bones.) Shell the shrimp, set the meat aside, and reserve the shells.

Put the heads, tails, and shells (and bones, if you filleted the fish) in a saucepan with no more than 1 quart of water and 1 teaspoon salt. Bring to a boil. Cover, reduce the heat, and simmer for 15 minutes.

Remove from heat and strain the resulting broth. Add the broth to the sauce and peppers. Dissolve the saffron in a ¼ cup of hot water and add to the soup. Bring to a low boil and add the squid. When the pot returns to a boil, add the shrimp. Bring to a boil again, and add the fish chunks and the mussels. Cover and cook about 3 minutes, or until the mussels have opened. Add salt to taste.

Give the pot a slow stir and sprinkle with chopped parsley. Serve with toasted bread.

Campania

Escarole and Chicory Soup
Zuppa di scarola e cicoria

Salerno's Green Bean Soup
Zuppa di fagiolini alla salernitana

Lentil, Celery, and Tomato Soup
Zuppa di lenticchie al pomodoro

Neapolitan Cabbage, Rice, and Cheese Soup
Minestra alla napoletana

Zucchini, Cheese, and Egg Soup
Minestra di zucchini, cacio e uova

Pasta and Squash Soup
Minestra di cocozza

Pasta and Potato Soup
Minestra di pasta e patate

Vegetable and Mussel Soup
Zuppa di verdure e cozze

Campania

By tracing an ideal line west to east—from the Gulf of Gaeta on the Tyrrhenian Sea to Vasto on the Adriatic—we would be drawing the equivalent of a Mason-Dixon line: Every land below it is the "Italian South." In Campania, the first region below the line, the pale, chalky northern light of the Settentrione is filtered through the golden warmth of a midday sun, when even the shadows reflect sunshine. Here everything grows lavishly: Mediterranean umbrellifera pines, subtropical aloe, tropical cactus, flaming bougainvillea, and wild orange blossoms; the ornate white flowers of the caper bloom from every crack in ancient walls or among tormented black volcanic stones; fig trees grow wild; orange, lemon, and olive groves thrive on the most fertile soil.

Campania, just south of Lazio and Molise, descends from the Apennines and stretches beside the blue, sparkling Tyrrhenian Sea along one of the most famously romantic coastlines in the world. The Gulf of Gaeta is the overture, the opening act for the unique opera to follow: The promontory of Pozzuoli and the islands of Procida and Ischia gaze from the left wing of the big stage that is the Gulf of Naples, which closes its half-moon sweep on the right with Sorrento's promontory pointing at the island of Capri. In the middle of the backdrop is Mount Vesuvius, the murderous volcano now coiled at rest and purring like a domesticated feline, a puff of white smoke over its head like a thought drawn in a cartoon. The volcano overlooks the magnificent bay, the whole nestled city of Naples, and what is left of once prosperous Pompeii. Around the bend from Sorrento comes Positano, clinging improbably to the precipitous cliffs, and then Amalfi and Ravello and finally Salerno. Along the Gulf of Salerno, the coastline takes a breather of flatland: thirty miles of blue sea on one side and a red sea of tomato plants and vineyards on the other, all the way to the ruins of Paestum. There convene all the aromas of Campania—wild oregano, basil, mint, asphodel, roses and carnations, cypresses, oleanders and eucalyptus. They barely make room for the stones of the ancient city and its old, majestic Greek temples to Neptune and Ceres. Next comes the Cilento coast, pushing south to reach in eighty miles the end of Campania at Sapri.

No wonder that Campania, the ancient Greek colony taken over by the Romans, and then the Normans, the Spanish, and the French, was always a traded, exchanged, or fought-over and most desirable piece of real estate. Ischia and Capri were the rich playgrounds of Roman emperors who built palatial residences there; following their lead, the aristocracy dotted the shores and the immediate inland with sumptuous villas. A few miles inland northeast of Naples at Caserta, Charles III, the Bourbon king, built his royal palace, a miniature Versailles—park, fountains, waterfall, and all. Now the islands and the Amalfi coast are the playground of old and new aristocracy, of the richly famous or the simply rich.

Campania has historically been among the most populous regions of Italy, a fact that has created a social pyramid in which the poorer masses support a privileged aristocracy at the very top. It makes for a class-conscious society, where titles have the social weight of currency and where appearance is frequently traded for substance. The have-nots and the underdogs, throughout the centuries, have genetically become the most cunningly witty survivors. They make a profession of survival, dedicated to the appreciation of life and continuously seeking the possibility of improvement, yet accepting with stoic good humor whatever life dishes out. They see the glass of life as half full and not as half empty; but then if really empty, they rejoice at the simple possession of the glass.

The Campani, with the Neapolitans leading, are generous to a fault; conscious that sooner or later they may well depend on the generosity of others, they share whatever they have—including work. They refuse to be labeled lazy: They have, as they will assure you, a dedicated, sentimental appreciation for all that is beautiful—and free, such as a ray of sunshine in winter or a sparkle of green-blue sea. It is a philosophy that engenders the beau geste, the better if flamboyant. The dialect of Campania is a musical instrument as much as a language. The spoken vocabulary and the construction of a phrase are used with the same abandon and inspiration as the plucking of a guitar. It is no coincidence that Naples is the birthplace of bel canto, the cultivated art of singing. It is from the heart of Naples that "O Sole Mio," "Funiculi 'Funicula,'" "Torna a Sorrento," "Marechiaro," and myriad other songs, exultant and sad—like thousands upon thousands of Italian emigrants—left the port of Naples to enrich the world.

It is in Campania that the little-appreciated *pomo d'oro* (as at first the tomato was called in Italy: "golden apple") from the New World was finally given deserved consideration and turned from a decorative (and "poisonous"!) element into a basic staple of the local cuisine. With the intensive use of the tomato, the Neapolitans changed Italy's—and in large measure the world's—

gastronomy. The tomato is still a basic crop of the region, and its canning a major industry. In Campania pastas developed their full potential and became a national flag, an art form, a leading entry in the encyclopedia of today's international foods.

The same pedigree is valid for pizza: When or why some Neapolitan baker felt the urge to squash a few tomatoes on a thin disk of bread dough, moisten it with a few drops of golden Campanian olive oil (no cheese, please), and slip the humble production in a hot oven is not recorded. While in the kitchens of the nobles, at the top of the pyramid, talented *monsiù* (Neapolitan for "chef") concocted fabled creations of pheasants and thrushes' tongues to compete with the best of European courts, it is at the base of the pyramid that the cuisine of Campania takes its identity.

The joyfulness, the exuberant resourcefulness of the people in making the best of everything—whatever much or little at hand—is what makes their table different. A meal may be made and gleefully appreciated out of the cornucopia that the land and the sea supply. But also a few Gaeta black olives and a soup made of old bread, water, and a few drops of olive oil may become a meal on an appreciative table. Add a few more olives, a few more drops of oil, a half-full glass of Falerno wine, a few friends, and it is a banquet.

Throw in a song, and it is a feast.

Escarole and Chicory Soup

Zuppa di scarola e cicoria

Cicoria is the name given to small, tender, and quite bitter wild dandelion greens, of which the small white root is the most sought-after part. Market chicory or dandelion greens can be used without altering the soup.

1½ pounds escarole

1½ pounds chicory

1 cup water

1 teaspoon salt

3 garlic cloves

½ cup olive oil

3 hot Italian-style sausages, skinned and crumbled

½ cup grated pecorino Romano cheese

6 to 12 slices Italian-style bread, oven-toasted

Wash the escarole and chicory several times to be absolutely sure that they are rid of dirt or sand. Shake dry and chop coarsely. In a pot large enough to contain the greens boil the water and salt and add the greens. Stir, cover, and cook over high heat until the greens are limp. Drain and squeeze dry, reserving all the liquid in the pot.

In a soup pot, sauté the garlic in the olive oil until the garlic is golden. Add the skinned and crumbled sausages, and brown over low heat, stirring constantly. Add the drained greens, and stir. Add the reserved cooking water (pass it through a fine sieve if necessary), stir, and bring to a boil. Add enough warm water to bring the contents of the pot to about 8 cups. Simmer for another 4 to 5 minutes, and stir in the cheese.

Serve hot with the toasted bread and additional grated cheese.

Salerno's Green Bean Soup

Zuppa di fagiolini alla salernitana

In a soup pot over medium heat, sauté the minced garlic and onion and the chopped hot pepper in the olive oil until the pepper begins to take on color. Add the tomatoes; stir and mash the tomatoes, and cook for about 15 minutes at a low boil, until the mixture resembles a chunky and thick tomato sauce.

Add the green beans, stir well, and, if needed, add enough water to cover. Add salt and pepper to taste, cover, and cook at a very low boil until the beans are tender, stirring once or twice.

Moisten the bread slices with a few drops of olive oil, oven-toast them, and distribute the oven-toasted bread slices among the serving dishes.

When the beans are tender, stir in the chopped basil, and serve.

2 garlic cloves, minced

1 small onion, minced

1 fresh hot pepper pod, chopped

⅛ cup olive oil

1½ pounds fresh plum tomatoes, peeled and chopped

1½ pounds fresh green beans, cut in 1- to 1½-inch lengths

Salt

Pepper

6 to 7 leaves fresh basil, minced

6 to 12 slices Italian-style bread

Lentil, Celery, and Tomato Soup

Zuppa di lenticchie al pomodoro

1 pound dried lentils

8 cups water

1½ teaspoons salt

3 cloves garlic, skewered on
  wooden toothpicks

3 celery ribs, cut in 2-inch
  sections

½ pound fresh plum tomatoes,
  peeled and chopped

3 tablespoons minced flat-leaf
  parsley

3 tablespoons minced fresh basil
  leaves

½ teaspoon powdered cayenne
  pepper

½ cup olive oil

1 loaf Italian-style bread, oven-
  warmed

Soak the dried lentils in enough cold water to cover for at least 2 hours. Drain the lentils and put them in a soup pot with about 8 cups water and the salt. Add the garlic and the celery, cover the pot, and bring it to a boil. Simmer for about 20 minutes, stirring occasionally, until the lentils are almost tender. Discard the garlic cloves.

In a small saucepan over high heat, sauté the tomatoes, parsley, basil, and cayenne pepper in the olive oil, stirring and mashing the tomatoes with a wooden spoon. Cook for 5 minutes, or until the tomatoes have reduced and thickened into a loose sauce. Add to the lentils, stir well, and cook until the lentils are tender.

The soup should be rather thick but still soupy. Let rest a few minutes, stir, and serve with oven-warmed bread.

Neapolitan Cabbage, Rice, and Cheese Soup

Minestra alla napoletana

In this recipe, provolone, Parmesan, and pecorino Romano cheese contribute to make a simple cabbage-and-rice soup a cheese lover's dish.

Core the cabbage, and remove and discard the tough outside leaves. Chop the remaining leaves coarsely, wash them, and shake them dry.

In a soup pot over high heat, sauté the minced salt pork, garlic, and onion in the olive oil until the onion is golden and limp. Add the chopped cabbage and the salt; cook and stir until the cabbage is limp. Add the water, and bring to a boil. Cover the pot and simmer for about 20 minutes, or until the cabbage is very tender. (At this stage, if needed, add some warm water to have about 8 cups of soup in the pot.)

Stir in the rice and cook another 14 minutes, or until the rice is tender. Stir in the diced provolone and the grated Parmesan and Romano cheeses until well blended.

Serve immediately, with additional cheese, if desired.

2 pounds savoy (curly-leaf) cabbage

3 ounces lean salt pork, minced

1 garlic clove, minced

1 large onion, minced

2 tablespoons olive oil

2 teaspoons salt

6 cups water

¾ cup medium-grain rice

4 ounces provolone cheese, diced

3 tablespoons grated Parmesan cheese

3 tablespoons grated pecorino Romano cheese

Zucchini, Cheese, and Egg Soup

Minestra di zucchini, cacio e uova

4 ounces bacon

1 onion

3 tablespoons olive oil

6 small zucchini (approximately 1½ pounds)

7 to 8 cups hot water

Salt

Freshly ground pepper

3 large eggs

4 tablespoons grated pecorino Romano or Parmesan cheese

6 sprigs flat-leaf parsley, minced with stems removed

6 leaves basil, minced

6 to 12 slices Italian-style bread, oven-toasted

Cut the bacon in thin strips and the onion in very thin slivers. In a soup pot over low heat, sauté the bacon and onion in the olive oil until the onion is limp and the bacon has rendered its fat but is not crisp.

Cut off the ends of the zucchini, then cut the zucchini in strips and cut these again into small cubes. Add the zucchini to the sauté and cook them a few moments, stirring. Add the hot water and cook at a low boil for 5 to 8 minutes, or until the zucchini are tender but not overcooked.

In a small bowl, beat the eggs well with a fork, adding the cheese, parsley, and basil, and mix thoroughly.

Stir the egg mixture slowly into the zucchini soup. As soon as the mixture is blended, remove from the heat.

Divide the toasts among the serving dishes, ladle the soup over them, and serve.

Pasta and Squash Soup

Minestra di cocozza

Southern Italy produces a squash variously called *cucuzza* or *cocozza*, botanically known as Naples squash. It is similar to a summer crookneck squash on this side of the Atlantic, but a normal pumpkin will serve well as a substitute.

In a soup pot over medium heat, sauté the garlic in the olive oil. When the garlic is golden, remove it and add the squash or pumpkin, salt, and hot pepper. Sauté and stir, and add just enough water to cover the squash. Cover the pot, and bring it to a boil. Lower the heat and cook until the squash cubes have nearly dissolved.

While the squash cooks, bring to boil enough salted water to cook the pasta. Cook until the pasta is tender; drain thoroughly but reserve some of the cooking water.

Add the cooked pasta to the squash soup and, if needed, enough cooking water to total 8 cups of soup. Stir in the butter, if using, and the parsley.

Serve with Parmesan cheese.

3 garlic cloves

⅓ cup olive oil

2 pounds summer crookneck squash or pumpkin, peeled and cubed

2 teaspoons salt

Dash of ground hot pepper

10 ounces small pasta, such as cannolicchi or tubettini

3 tablespoons unsalted butter (optional)

4 tablespoons minced parsley

Parmesan cheese

Pasta and Potato Soup

Minestra di pasta e patate

Wherever there is a large consumption of pasta, as in southern Italy, there always remain a certain amount of different cuts of pasta, long and short, which by themselves are not enough for a dish. These remainders, called *rimanenze* in some regions and *munnezzaglia* ("small garbage") in Campania, are pooled together and used for soups, imparting an interesting texture. Sometimes the *munnezzaglia* is created on purpose by breaking up and mixing different cuts of pasta.

3 to 4 ounces fat from salt pork or prosciutto, minced

1 large onion, minced

1 carrot, peeled and minced

2 celery ribs, minced

6 sprigs flat-leaf parsley, minced with stems removed

4 tablespoons olive oil

2 pounds potatoes, peeled and cubed

4 fresh plum tomatoes, peeled and crushed

Salt

Freshly grated pepper

8 cups hot water or chicken broth

10 ounces mixed small cuts of pasta, such as tubettini, ditalini, or bow ties

½ cup freshly grated Parmesan cheese

In a soup pot over moderate heat, sauté the minced salt pork fat, onion, carrot, celery, and parsley in the olive oil. When the mince has started to color, add the potatoes, tomatoes, and salt and pepper to taste.

Add one cup of the water or broth, and mix well. Cover the pot and cook over low to medium heat for about 30 minutes, stirring occasionally.

Bring the remaining water or broth to a boil and add to the potato mixture. Boil for 1 to 2 minutes. If a thicker soup is desired, scoop out a few potato pieces, mash them, and set aside.

Add the pasta to the boiling pot and cook until the thickest of the pasta cuts is tender. Stir in the mashed potato, if using.

Remove the pot from the heat, add the cheese, stir, and allow to rest a moment or two. Serve with more grated cheese, if desired.

Vegetable and Mussel Soup

Zuppa di verdure e cozze

Clean and scrub the mussels, and set them aside in a bowl of cold water.

Clean, wash, and prepare the vegetables, chopping them coarsely together. In a soup pot with 2½ quarts of lightly salted water, bring the vegetables to a boil and simmer uncovered until all the vegetables are well cooked and the soup has thickened.

In a small saucepan, sauté the minced basil, parsley, rosemary, and garlic in the olive oil until the garlic is golden. Add the sautéed mince to the soup pot.

Scoop the mussels out of the water and into a large pot, cover, and raise the heat until the mussels open, about 4 to 5 minutes. Scoop out the mussels with a slotted spoon, letting their juices fall into the pot. While the mussels cool, strain the remaining liquids through a fine sieve into the vegetable soup. Remove the mussels from their shells and add the meats to the soup. Add salt and pepper to taste.

Divide the toasts among the serving dishes, and ladle the mussel soup over them. No cheese, please.

4 pounds mussels

3 pounds mixed seasonable vegetables, such as zucchini, onion, Swiss chard, spinach, celery, potato, turnip, or carrot

5 to 6 leaves fresh basil, minced

3 to 4 sprigs flat-leaf parsley, minced

1 sprig fresh rosemary, minced

1 garlic clove, minced

⅓ cup olive oil

6 to 12 slices of Italian-style bread, oven-toasted

Puglia

Foggia's Potato and Fennel Soup
Simmuledda alla foggiana

Escarole, Chicory, Celery, and Fennel Soup
Minestra maritata alla pugliese

Dandelion, Red Onion, and Fava Soup
Minestra di fava, cicoriella e cipolle

Onion and Potato Soup
Cialda ricca

Pasta and Chickpea Soup, Lecce Style
Minestra di lasagnette e ceci alla leccese

Orecchiette and Swiss Chard in Fish Broth
Orecchiette in brodo di pesce

Rice and Potato Soup with Mussels
Tiella alla pugliese

Apulian Pasta and Bean Soup with Mussels
Minestra di pasta e fagioli e cozze

Puglia

There is a definite difference between Apulia (Puglia) and the other regions of Italy: With Apulia, it is not love at first sight. You will start giving in to the unusual allure of the land and the sea slowly. Then Apulia will grow on you.

You will know immediately when you are in the bleached land of Apulia, an old, tired land, its face and body powdered by dust, a land reminiscent of a sunbaked Mesopotamia without Tigris or Euphrates. Apulia does not have any rivers at all, or anything that could reasonably be called such; rainfall is scarce, the lowest in Italy, a fact that justifies the region's name—*A-pluvia,* Latin for "absence of rain."

The traveler's first impression of the land is of flatness. The *Tavoliere* is one of the largest plains of peninsular Italy, covering a great part of the region, from its bony western Apennine border to the sea. Once a deadly malarial swamp from which people either fled or died, it was slowly reclaimed and turned into modern Italy's largest wheat basket, a miniature Kansas.

At the edge of the plain, here and there the land rises in tentative "mountains," gritty and dried out, and the calcareous sandstone moves south all along to form the hilly central part of Apulia, finally to pile up into the Murge Mountains. The region graduates into the Salento, the stiletto heel of the Italian boot dipping into the Ionian Sea. From prehistory on, weather, nature, and man in unholy allegiance have stripped the region naked of any major woods, leaving the land shorn, letting the Mediterranean *macchia,* the brushwood, grow wherever it can. Only here and there are more recent clumps of woods, samples of what it could have been.

In the region's north, the Gargano juts into the Adriatic Sea forming the spur of the boot. It rises in steep, barren gradients from the flat earth and, on three sides, plunges almost vertically into the sea. The promontory's difficult access segregated it from the rest of the land and made it the repository of mythical, mysterious legends. Supposedly the residence of malicious spirits and generous gods, the land played host to prophets and oracles who camped there in sacred caves and erected temples to which pilgrimages were made, seeking protection or assistance.

East toward the sea, the Gargano becomes gentler and rounder and—surprise!—green with groves of huge olive trees, oaks, chestnuts, and pine. At the bottom of the cliffs nest colorful fishing villages of ancient origin: Rodi Garganico, Peschici, Vieste, and Mattinata have now become fashionable resorts. It seems fitting that the spirits of fun and the gods of fashion are replacing the scary and austere deities of old.

Where the Gargano ends, the rest of Apulia begins: Facing south, a flat blue sea is at the left, and flat land rests everywhere else. There you begin to see elements of a rich, fabulous past. West and south of here extends the Daunia, a province settled, legend says, by the Homeric hero Diomedes. Upon his death, his followers were transformed by the gods into *diomedee* birds—albatrosses—so they could mournfully glide and circle over his tomb, protecting it. They still fly high today, with hundreds of other species, in the bird sanctuary of the Gargano.

Forty miles to the west is Foggia, a city of Norman origins, that has been destroyed, rebuilt, pillaged, plundered, and rebuilt again by the Longobards, the French, the Spanish, the Saracens, by princes, emperors, bishops, and popes—in 1731, even an earthquake managed to knock it down. Foggia is today a flourishing commercial agricultural center and—no wonder—the Foggiani are the most guardedly optimistic, and resilient, of people. Each event has left its mark, visible in the various temples, churches, palaces, and urban monuments. In the Middle Ages, Emperor Frederick II—king of Germany, king of Sicily, king of Jerusalem—loved Apulia and left official buildings behind, most imposing of all the Castel del Monte, a massive octagonal structure rising on top of a hillock like an enormous, geometrical rock sprouted from the earth, its eight elegantly naked towers looking out over the blank wheat plains that surround it.

A bit southeast of Foggia is Cannae, the *Tavoliere* site where in 216 B.C. Hannibal and his Carthaginians crushed the Roman army, possibly the most humiliating defeat in Roman history. Every stone of the land appears to be a marker of history, from prehistoric burial *dolmen* and *menhirs* to the pockmarks of World War II. Because Apulia's geographical position makes it the bridgehead between north and central Europe and the Levant, the Romans built the Appian Way from Rome to the ports of Taranto and Brindisi, the "doors to the Orient." For the better part of two millennia it carried across Apulia all the traffic of goods and cultures to and from the North and East. Today a large part of the traffic is carried by the port of Bari, capital and nerve center of the region; a large metropolis, it is also a cultural center, known for its universities, museums, and theaters of national importance.

Not too far south is the unique Alberobello and its immediate surroundings dotted with more than 1,000 *trulli,* unique white round stone houses with black, conical roofs put together without mortar. As a final surprise, at the heel of the boot is Lecce, a city largely of one style, baroque. Emperor Charles V of Aragon started the reconstructive spurt by building around the city a defensive wall against the marauding Turks. The sixteenth, seventeenth, and eighteenth centuries saw the city become what is considered one of the world's capitals of baroque art.

Apulia has been a land of transit—Greeks, Romans, Normans, Longobards, Spaniards, Swabian Germans, Turks—and yet it has a unified character. The local cuisine reflects this trait; only minor differences are encountered from one province to another. Tomatoes, peppers, eggplants, and local wild field greens and herbs spiked by invention and inspiration make for the colorful Apulian table. The harvest of the sea and of the land—foremost, pasta made simply with the local hard wheat and water, as in the famous orecchiette—are the basic staples, often coupled together, as in "Mussel, Bean, and Pasta Soup," or "Pasta, Vegetables, and Fish Broth Soup." Apulians are particularly proud of their now extensively cultivated olive trees and the resulting oil, scented and thick. The abundant, sturdy Apulian grapes, once grown to cut and give body to refined foreign wines, are now producing—with the help of modern know-how—some remarkable Sauvignons and Chardonnays.

Once the attentive traveler has absorbed what this region is, has partaken of its food and its wine, then he will see Apulia's nature with different, more generous eyes.

And love at second sight is more permanent.

Foggia's Potato and Fennel Soup

Simmuledda alla foggiana

The title should read "wild fennel soup," but wild fennel, which grows in Apulian fields, is not available here. Wild fennel looks similar to dill but has a strong anise flavor and aroma. Substituting a fennel bulb gives a worthwhile version of the characteristic soup from Foggia.

1 fennel bulb

6 cups beef broth

1 pound potatoes, peeled and sliced thin

6 tablespoons coarse semolina flour or instant polenta flour

Grated Parmesan cheese

Remove and discard the coarse outside leaves and stems from the fennel bulb. Save the feathery top leaves and chop coarsely. Cut the bulb in quarters, core it, separate the leaves, and slice as thinly as possible with a vegetable peeler.

In a soup pot, bring the broth to a boil and add the sliced fennel and potatoes and the chopped fennel leaves. Simmer until the potatoes are quite soft, about 5 to 10 minutes.

In a small bowl, dilute the flour in enough cold water to obtain a smooth, thin batter. Return the broth to a boil and stir the batter into it. Cook at a low boil, stirring occasionally, for 15 minutes (5 minutes if using the polenta).

Serve topped with grated Parmesan cheese.

Escarole, Chicory, Celery, and Fennel Soup

Minestra maritata alla pugliese

Wash carefully and trim as necessary the escarole and chicory. In a soup pot, cook the greens in enough salted water to cover. Drain well and chop the greens coarsely.

Trim the celery and cut in 1½-inch pieces.

Remove the stems and tough outside leaves from fennel bulb; cut the bulb in quarters, core it, and cut the remaining fennel in thin slices.

Put celery and fennel in a pot with enough salted water to cover, and boil until tender, about 10 minutes. Drain and mix well with the chopped greens.

In a large pot, bring the broth to a boil.

Cut the salt pork in small cubes and add to the boiling broth. In an ovenproof casserole or soup tureen, make a layer of the mixed vegetables, cover with a generous sprinkling of cheese, and a few dashes of pepper. Ladle in some of the hot broth, and repeat the layering until all the ingredients are used, finishing with the cheese. Let the soup rest.

Before serving, warm the oven to 400°F and heat the soup in the tureen for 4 to 5 minutes, and serve.

1½ pounds escarole

1½ pounds chicory

1 pound celery

1 pound fennel

6 cups beef broth

4 ounces salt pork

5 ounces grated pecorino Romano cheese

Fresh ground pepper

Dandelion, Red Onion, and Fava Soup

Minestra di fava, cicoriella e cipolle

Almost like a ritual of spring in all regions of Italy is the common sight of people in fields, on roadsides, and at public parks, picking wild *cicoria,* the dandelion green, before it flowers. Most sought-after is *cicoriella,* the youngest and most tender. Popular belief gives medicinal properties to the bitterish weed and its tiny white root, considering it a tonic with beneficial effects, especially for the liver.

1½ pounds dried fava beans

8 cups water

3 teaspoons salt

1½ pounds dandelion greens

½ cup olive oil

2 red onions (1½ pounds, approximate), cut in thin slivers

Extra-virgin olive oil

Soak the dried fava beans overnight in enough water to cover. Drain the soaked beans and add to a soup pot with the 8 cups water and 2 teaspoons of the salt. Bring to a boil, and partially cover the pot. Lower the heat and simmer, stirring occasionally, for 1 hour, or until the fava beans are very well cooked and practically fall apart. Mash the beans with a wooden spoon, forming a rough puree.

While the beans cook, wash the dandelion greens several times until they are free of any dirt or sand; shake them dry. Put the greens in a second pot with only the water that clings to them, and add the remaining 1 teaspoon salt. Cover and cook for 15 minutes, stirring once or twice. Drain the greens in a colander and squeeze dry. Chop the greens coarsely, stir them into the fava soup, and let simmer gently for about 10 minutes.

Soak the onion slivers in enough cold water to cover for 15 to 20 minutes, changing the water a few times. Drain thoroughly and stir the onions into the soup. When well-mixed, remove the pot from the heat. Serve with a dribble of extra-virgin olive oil on the individual serving dishes, if so desired.

Onion and Potato Soup

Cialda ricca

In a soup pot over medium heat, sauté the anchovies, garlic, and red pepper pods in the olive oil until the anchovies have nearly dissolved. (You may retrieve and discard the garlic now, but this is a long-cooking soup, and the garlic will boil away.) Discard the red pepper pods.

Increase the heat, and add the onions, tomatoes, and potatoes to the soup pot. Stir well, cooking for 1 to 2 minutes. Add the broth, and bring to a boil. Cover the pot partially, reduce the heat, and simmer for 45 minutes, stirring occasionally, or until all is very well cooked, with barely a trace of texture.

Divide the dried bread among the serving dishes. Sprinkle with the oregano, chopped basil, and freshly ground pepper, pour the hot soup over it, and serve.

4 anchovy filets, chopped

2 garlic cloves

1 to 2 red pepper pods

½ cup olive oil

1 pound onions, cut in thin slivers

1 pound fresh plum tomatoes, peeled and chopped

½ pound potatoes, cut in very fine slices or matchsticks

4 tablespoons chopped flat-leaf parsley

8 cups chicken broth or water salted with 2 teaspoons salt

6 to 12 slices dried-out whole wheat bread (page 262)

2 tablespoons oregano

5 to 6 fresh basil leaves, chopped (optional)

Freshly ground pepper

Pasta and Chickpea Soup, Lecce Style

Minestra di lasagnette e ceci alla leccese

7 cups water or beef broth

1 pound (approximate) canned chickpeas, undrained

6 anchovy filets

3 to 4 garlic cloves

2 to 3 sprigs fresh rosemary

½ cup olive oil

10 ounces lasagnette (Apulian homemade pasta, page 259), cut slightly larger than fettuccine and 3 to 4 inches long)

In a soup pot, bring the broth to a boil. Add ¾ of the canned chickpeas and their canning liquid to the pot. Mash the remaining chickpeas, and add to the pot. Stir, reduce the heat, and simmer for 10 minutes.

In the meantime, mash the anchovies and garlic into a paste. In a small saucepan, sauté the anchovy-garlic paste and the rosemary in the olive oil until the rosemary looks fried. Remove from heat and allow to cool. Remove and discard the rosemary sprigs.

Stir the oil into the soup pot, and return the mixture to a boil. Add the lasagnette, and cook until the pasta is tender. Serve immediately.

Orecchiette and Swiss Chard in Fish Broth

Orecchiette in brodo di pesce

In a large pot, bring 2 quarts lightly salted water to a boil and add the onion, carrot, celery, and parsley. Cover and simmer for 10 minutes.

Clean and scale the bass, and add to the pot whole with the wine vinegar. Reduce the heat and simmer slowly for 8 minutes. Scoop out the fish with a slotted spoon and set aside.

Strain the fish cooking liquid with a sieve into a soup pot, and bring the liquid to a boil. Add the Swiss chard, cooking until it turns limp; then add the potato and the orecchiette. Cook for 8 to 10 minutes, or until the pasta is done.

(For a one-dish meal, add to the soup the meat of the reserved fish, cut in pieces, or save the fish for another use.)

Serve the soup warm with shreds of pecorino Romano cheese.

Note: This soup may be made with fish broth (see page 255). In this case, omit the onion, carrot, celery, parsley, sea bass, and wine vinegar, and cook the chard, potato, and orecchiette in the boiling fish broth.

1 onion

1 carrot

1 celery rib

4 sprigs flat-leaf parsley

2 small sea bass (1½ to 2 pounds approximate)

2 tablespoons red wine vinegar

1½ pounds Swiss chard, coarsely chopped

1 small potato, peeled and grated

1 batch homemade orecchiette, page 260, (or 8 ounces commercial fresh pasta)

Shredded pecorino Romano cheese

Rice and Potato Soup with Mussels

Tiella alla pugliese

2½ pounds mussels

½ cup olive oil

Dash of freshly ground pepper

½ cup dry white wine

3 to 4 ounces salt pork, minced

1 small onion, minced

1 garlic clove, minced

1 pound potatoes, peeled and
   cubed

8 cups water

1 teaspoon salt

1 cup long-grain rice

Wash and scrub the mussels, and soak them in enough cold water to cover. Drain. In a large pan over high heat, sauté the mussels in ¼ cup of the olive oil with the pepper. Cover the pan, and cook until the mussels open (discard the ones that do not). Add the wine, and cover the pot. When the wine has steamed away, remove the pan from the heat and scoop the mussels out, letting the juice fall into the pan, reserving all the liquid. When the mussels are cool, remove the meat and set aside.

In a soup pot, sauté the minced salt pork, onion, and garlic in the remaining ¼ cup of olive oil until the mince is limp and golden.

Add the potatoes, and stir. Add the water and salt, and bring the pot to a boil for 10 minutes. Add the rice and cook at a low boil for 14 minutes, stirring occasionally.

Just before removing the pot from the heat, strain the reserved mussel liquid and add it with the mussel meat to the soup pot. Stir carefully; the soup should be reasonably thick but soupy. If too thin, let rest a while; the rice and potato will thicken. If too thick, stir in some warm water.

Serve hot or lukewarm. Do not reheat.

Apulian Pasta and Bean Soup with Mussels

Minestra di pasta e fagioli e cozze

Clean and scrub the mussels, and soak in enough cold water to cover for at least 30 minutes. In a large pan over high heat, sauté the drained mussels in ¼ cup of the olive oil. Cover, and when all the mussels have opened (discard the ones that do not), add the wine and cover immediately. When the wine has nearly evaporated, scoop out the mussels, letting all the juice fall into the pan, reserving all the liquid. Remove the meat from the shells, and set aside.

In a soup pot, bring the fish broth and the salted water to a boil. Add all the beans' canning water, and half the beans. Mash the remaining half and add to the broth.

Strain the reserved mussel liquid into the broth, and cook for 1 to 2 minutes, stirring. Add the pasta and cook at a lively boil until the pasta is tender.

In a small saucepan over medium heat, sauté the garlic, red pepper, and rosemary in the remaining ¼ cup olive oil until the garlic is lightly browned. Allow to cool, then strain the flavored oil through a sieve into the soup. Add the mussel meat, stir, remove the pot from the heat, and let rest 1 minute.

Serve hot or lukewarm, but do not reheat.

2½ pounds mussels

½ cup olive oil

½ cup white dry wine

3 cups canned Roman beans, undrained

4 cups fish broth (page 255), or made from bouillon cubes)

5 cups lightly salted water

10 ounces egg fettucine, broken in pieces

2 garlic cloves

1 to 2 dried red pepper pods

1 sprig rosemary

Calabria

Asparagus Soup from Sila
Minestra di asparagi silana

Calabrian Onion Soup
Zuppa di cipolla alla calabrese

Potato and Onion Soup
Licurdia

Fava and Endive Soup
Minestra di fave e indivia

Calabrian Celery Soup
Zuppa d'accia

"A Thousand Little Things" Soup
Millecosedde

Calabrian Bread Soup
Pancotto alla calabrese

Bread Pancake Soup
Mariola

Swordfish and Cabbage Soup
Minestra di pescespada e cavolo

Calabria

Calabria, straddling two seas, forms the tip of the Italian boot: The toe dips into the Tyrrhenian, the instep rests in the Ionic. The land has an amazingly varied beauty. The Tyrrhenian coast is all high rocky cliffs, mini bays and coves; the Ionic coast is a continuous stretch of 150 miles of white sandy beach. Between the two is where the Apennine Mountains, having ranged the whole length of Italy, come to die on the doorstep of Sicily. The Appennino Calabro is a complex massif that makes up most of the region's territory: Of the region's 409 counties, 387 are considered mountain localities.

The inviting, defenseless coast made it easy for outsiders to come in and, once they had taken hold of the mountains, hard to budge them out. The Greeks established themselves and flourished there, calling this colony part of Magna Graecia. One of its cities, Sybaris, became so rich as an exchange center of precious goods that its opulent citizens, the Sybarites, went down in history as luxurious people, abnormally fond of refined pleasures.

During the second and third centuries B.C., in the worst possible political decision, Calabria sided with the loser in the Punic Wars. Carthage was defeated, and Rome shaped the destiny of Calabria for the centuries to come. Many future Roman fleets were built with Calabrian wood (the process left much of the land treeless, with all related consequences). But the real social scourge established by the Romans was the *latifondo,* the division of the land into a few large holdings. The absentee owners of the huge farms enslaved the native workers with nearly no entitlements, a practice lasting to the 1950s, when the large holdings were split and distributed to small farmers. Around the beginning of the twentieth century, the demand for labor in the Americas and Australia opened the door of the Calabrian cage: A very high percentage of the region's able men, women, and children fled the land in the first big wave of emigrants. Enormous progress has been made since then, bringing changes that began to be apparent within the last fifty years. With the new exposure, the image of Calabria as a parched, stark land is now beginning to be set aside, and like the peeling of the seven veils, its cultural and natural beauties are revealed.

The highlands of La Sila, the central part of the region, are a succession of green mountains, once again covered with maple, pine, and fir forests and dotted with artificial and natural mountain lakes. The Ionic side, from foothills stretching almost to the sea, is now a wall-to-wall carpet of vineyards and olive groves. Calabria's flora, preserved in its national parks, are a botanist's dream come true; in winter, just above Cosenza there is skiing, while a few miles west, snorkeling and swimming go on from spring to October or November.

New interest has piqued archeology, and finds of inestimable value continue to surface from the earth and the sea. The Riace Bronzes, the six-foot-two-inch bronze statues of two Greek athletes, were fished from the Ionian Sea about thirty years ago. The bronzes are now exhibited in the Museum of the Magna Graecia, and many say they alone are worth a trip to Calabria.

Traveling down the Tyrrhenian coast, every twist and turn, every stop along the way, is worth the effort—even the final encounter with the mythological monsters of Scylla and Charybdis. Facing each other, as Homer tells it, they torment and toss the weary voyager back and forth in a gauntlet of terror and, finally, devour him in churning waters. Today, face to face, the monsters are a letdown, to say the least. Scylla is a delightfully quiet village, perched high over a long sandy beach; Charybdis is nowhere in sight, hiding somewhere in the same sea navigated by Odysseus. From Scylla, the sunny tip of Sicily can be seen at the other side of the Straits of Messina, and perhaps old Charybdis is poised there, in retirement.

On the gastronomical scene, this proximity to Sicily points out how the Calabrian table is made by the culinary influences of its neighbors and by shaded memories of past colonizers, especially Greece. Evident reminders are the *licurdia,* a spicy onion soup, daughter of the Apulian *ncapriata* soup, and the *minestra di fave e indivia,* a soup of fava beans and endive, an elaborate version of the Sicilian *maccu* soup. The Calabrian menu is heavy on soups that seem to copy other regions' entries: pasta and beans, pasta and chickpeas, onion soup, pasta and fava beans, fava and chicory. Not particularly original to the region is the traditional use of pasta made only with semolina flour and water, almost as if eggs were considered a rich item, and egg pasta a prerogative of the landlord's table.

The Calabrian cuisine could be thought of as not particularly inspiring, but—silver lining to grayish clouds—it has been central to the recent studies of the "Mediterranean diet." It has been deemed exemplary of a healthy nutrition for its use of olive oil, hot peppers, beans, deep green vegetables, cabbage, whole wheat, and hard wheat. Actually, what has been left out of the equation is that the Calabrian cuisine, as an essay by the Academy of Calabrian Foods and Wines describes it, is "not a poor cuisine but a cuisine of poor people."

Asparagus Soup from Sila

Minestra di asparagi silana

The Sila is the beautiful mountainous, wooded highland at the geographical center of Calabria. Among the many edible specialties of the Sila are the tiny wild asparagus. A close approximation can be obtained by snatching the first thin asparagus of the season as soon as it appears on the market.

Wash the asparagus carefully and break off the lower stem where it snaps off easily. Cut off and set aside the 1- to 1½-inch-long green tips.

Peel the lower stems, chop them coarsely, and put them in a soup pot with the chicken broth. Bring to a boil, and cook for 10 to 15 minutes, or until the stem pieces are very tender. Allow to cool, then pass the pieces and the broth through a food mill or press through a sieve, collecting the puree in a pot. Bring the puree to a boil, add the reserved asparagus tips, and cook 2 to 3 minutes, or until tender but still crisp. Scoop the tips out from the broth with a slotted spoon and set aside.

In a casserole, sauté the garlic cloves and pepper pod in the ⅓ cup of olive oil until they begin to brown slightly. Discard garlic and pepper.

Whisk the flour into the oil and cook and stir until it becomes smooth and golden.

Whisk the flour mixture into the broth, and bring the pot to a low boil. Reduce the heat, and add the reserved cooked asparagus tips.

Add salt and freshly ground pepper to taste. Continue to cook over moderate heat for 2 to 3 minutes. Stir gently, and serve accompanied by toasted croutons, if desired.

1½ pounds wild asparagus spears

8 cups chicken broth

⅓ cup olive oil

3 garlic cloves, crushed

*1 red pepper pod, or powdered
   cayenne pepper to taste*

*¾ cup all-purpose unbleached
   flour*

Salt

Freshly ground pepper

Croutons (optional)

Calabrian Onion Soup

Zuppa di cipolla alla calabrese

Nearly every region of Italy has at least one version of onion soup; Calabria has two. What makes this a bit different from others—and out of the austere Calabrian mold—is a touch of sugar and a bit of grappa or, for less fiery tastes, dry marsala wine or sherry.

2½ pounds large onions, sliced thin

6 tablespoons olive oil

2 teaspoons salt

1 tablespoon sugar

8 cups beef broth

6 tablespoons grappa, or ¾ cup dry marsala or sherry

6 to 12 slices Italian-style bread, oven-toasted

Freshly grated pecorino Romano cheese

In a soup pot, sauté the onions in the olive oil until the onions are translucent and just barely beginning to brown. Add salt and the sugar. (If using the marsala or sherry, stir it in now.) In a large saucepan, heat the beef broth to boiling. Pour the broth slowly into the soup pot. Cover, reduce the heat, and simmer for about 25 minutes.

Stir in the grappa and cook another 5 minutes. Divide the toasted bread among the serving dishes, and ladle the onion soup over the top. Serve immediately with the grated cheese.

Potato and Onion Soup

Licurdia

Nearly every Calabrian village has its own version of *licurdia,* adding, subtracting, or changing the proportions of the different vegetables and ingredients. This version straddles the middle of the road.

Wash and peel the carrots and potatoes; trim and core the lettuce. Chop all the vegetables coarsely and place them in a soup pot. Add the water and the salt, and bring to a boil. Cover, reduce the heat, and simmer 45 minutes, or until the carrots and potatoes are very tender.

Slice the onions thinly; blanch the slices briefly in boiling water, and drain. Mince the salt pork to a paste. In a saucepan sauté the salt pork in the olive oil until it becomes translucent, then add the onion slices. Stir and cook until onions are limp. Add the wine and cook over high heat until the wine has nearly evaporated and the onions have become a sort of textured sauce.

Pass the cooked vegetables and their cooking liquids through a food mill or a sieve into another pot. Add the onion mixture, stir well, and warm to serving temperature over medium heat.

Rub the toasted bread with the opened red pepper pods (or dribble with a few drops of Tabasco). Divide the toasts among the soup plates, and ladle the soup over them. Sprinkle with the grated cheese, and serve.

½ pound carrots

1 pound potatoes

1 head Boston lettuce

10 cups water

2 teaspoons salt

1 pound onions

4 ounces salt pork

2 tablespoons olive oil

½ cup dry white wine (or, for a richer soup, dry marsala wine)

6 to 12 slices Italian-style bread, oven-toasted

Fresh red pepper pods, or Tabasco sauce to taste

Freshly grated pecorino Romano cheese

Fava and Endive Soup

Minestra di fave e indivia

1 pound shelled fresh fava beans
   (about 2 to 2½ pounds
   unshelled)

2 teaspoons salt

1 small onion, minced

2 red pepper pods, or ½ teaspoon
   powdered cayenne pepper

⅓ cup olive oil

2 pounds curly endive

6 cups beef broth

Freshly ground pepper

In a large pan, soak the fava beans in enough water to cover and 1 teaspoon of the salt. Cook for 30 minutes, or until the beans are very soft. Pass the beans and their cooking water through a food mill, or puree them in a food processor.

In a soup pot over medium heat, sauté the minced onion and pepper pods in the olive oil until the onion begins to color. Add the fava bean puree, mix well, and simmer for 1 to 2 minutes.

Wash the curly endive and shake dry. In a large pot, bring 1 cup of water and the remaining 1 teaspoon salt to a boil, and add the endive with only the water that clings to it. Cover and cook for 10 minutes, or until the endive is tender. Drain well, chop coarsely, and add to the fava puree.

Slowly add the broth until the soup reaches a reasonably thick consistency. Add salt to taste. Sprinkle with freshly ground pepper to taste, and serve.

Calabrian Celery Soup

Zuppa d'accia

Wash the celery, peel away the toughest strings from the ribs, and cut the ribs in ½-inch slices. Boil in lightly salted water for 5 minutes; drain well.

In a skillet, sauté the sausages in 2 tablespoons of the olive oil until browned. Drain well, and allow to cool. In the same skillet, add the remaining 2 tablespoons olive oil, the celery, salt, and cayenne pepper, and sauté over high heat for 2 to 3 minutes.

In a soup pot, combine the sautéed celery and the broth, and bring to a boil.

Slice the cooked sausages in rounds. Cut the *soppressata* and the provolone in small strips or cubes, and the boiled eggs in wedges or rounds.

Divide the toasted bread, sausage rounds, *soppressata,* provolone, and boiled egg among the serving dishes. Ladle the hot celery broth over the top. Serve topped with grated cheese and freshly ground pepper.

1½ to 2 pounds celery ribs

2 Italian sweet sausages, about 4 to 5 ounces total

4 tablespoons olive oil

1 teaspoon salt

½ teaspoon powdered cayenne pepper

8 cups beef broth

4 ounces soppressata *salami*

4 to 5 ounces sharp provolone cheese

4 hard-boiled eggs

6 to 12 slices Italian-style bread, drizzled with olive oil and oven-toasted

Freshly grated pecorino Romano cheese

Freshly ground pepper

"A Thousand Little Things" Soup

Millecosedde

Millecosedde's translation as "a thousand little things" refers to the many legumes and vegetables that, like stars, revolve around the central sun: cubed pancetta or lean salt pork. The amount in this recipe has been decreased to adhere to modern nutrition rules, but in the traditional version, the meat quantity is almost double, in compliance with the great importance the table of Calabria gives to pork and all its products.

4 ounces dried fava beans

4 ounces dried cannellini beans

4 ounces dried chickpeas

4 ounces dried lentils

5 ounces pancetta or lean salt pork, cubed

2 tablespoons olive oil

1 small onion, chopped

1 celery rib, trimmed and chopped

1 carrot, peeled and chopped

2 garlic cloves, crushed

3 red pepper pods, or 1 teaspoon powdered cayenne pepper

10 cups water

2 teaspoons salt

1 potato, cubed

(Cont.)

Soak together the dried fava beans, cannellini, chickpeas, and lentils in enough cold water to cover for 24 hours. Drain.

In a soup pot, sauté in the olive oil the pancetta, onion, celery, carrot, garlic, and red pepper pods until the salt pork and onion are nearly translucent. Add the water, salt, and the drained legumes.

Bring to a boil, reduce the heat, and simmer for about 1½ hours, or until the sturdiest legumes are nearly tender. Add the potato, lettuce, cabbage, and mushrooms, and return the pot to a boil. Reduce the heat and simmer, uncovered, for 45 minutes. If the soup is too thick, add a little warm water.

In a separate pot, cook the pasta in lightly salted water. Drain, and add to the cooked soup. Add salt and pepper to taste. Serve warm or at room temperature, with freshly grated pecorino Romano cheese.

Note: You may substitute ¾ cup olive oil for the pancetta or salt pork.

½ *head romaine lettuce, cored and cut in strips*

½ *head small cabbage, cored and cut in strips*

5 to 6 fresh mushrooms, sliced

10 to 12 ounces small-cut macaroni, such as cannolicchi, elbows, pennette, and so on

Freshly grated pecorino Romano cheese

Calabrian Bread Soup

Pancotto alla calabrese

In a saucepan, sauté the garlic, red pepper pods, and bay leaves in the olive oil until garlic is lightly brown.

Add the celery, tomatoes, and salt; bring the pot to a low boil, and cook for 15 minutes. Remove and discard the garlic and bay leaves and add the bell pepper. Keep the soup warm over low heat; it should have a reasonably thick sauce consistency.

In a soup pot, bring the broth to a boil. Add the cubed bread, cover, and cook 15 minutes, or until the bread has nearly dissolved. Stir the sauce into the bread mixture, and cook for 1 minute.

Ladle the soup into the serving dishes (add the poached eggs, if using), and sprinkle with minced parsley just prior to serving.

3 cloves of garlic, crushed

2 red pepper pods, or ½ teaspoon powdered cayenne pepper

2 bay leaves

¼ *cup olive oil*

2 ribs celery, trimmed and sliced

1 pound ripe plum tomatoes, peeled, seeded, and chopped

2 teaspoons salt

1 green bell pepper, roasted, peeled, and sliced thin

8 cups hot beef broth

(Cont.)

8 to 12 ounces dried-out Italian-
style bread, cubed

6 poached eggs (optional)

2 to 3 tablespoons minced flat-
leaf parsley

Bread Pancake Soup

Mariola

The popular wisdom of "waste not, want not" is put to work in this soup, which is both delicate and sturdy. The sturdiness is supplied by the pancakes, made with remainders of old bread saved for this purpose, turned into bread crumbs, and mixed with the eggs.

4 eggs

⅓ cup unflavored bread crumbs

2 tablespoons minced fresh
parsley

2 tablespoons minced fresh
marjoram

½ teaspoon salt

Dash of cayenne pepper or
Tabasco sauce (optional)

Olive oil

8 cups beef broth

Freshly grated pecorino Romano
cheese

In a bowl, combine the eggs, bread crumbs, parsley, marjoram, salt, and cayenne pepper, if using. Mix well to create a thick but spoonable batter. (Do not let rest, as the bread crumbs tend to dry up the batter. If the batter is too thick or dry, add a little water or broth.)

Lightly oil a well-seasoned omelet pan or griddle, and pour the batter as for pancakes, the larger the better. (Do not make them thicker than ½ inch.) When golden on both sides, set aside and allow to cool.

Cut the pancakes in ½-inch (or slightly larger) strips and then into squares. Let the pieces dry a bit if you wish, and place them in a soup tureen.

In a soup pot, bring the broth to a boil. Add the boiling broth to the pancake squares in the soup tureen. Serve with freshly grated pecorino Romano cheese.

Swordfish and Cabbage Soup

Minestra di pescespada e cavolo

Swordfish is still snared in the waters near the Messina Straits—chased with fast, oar-propelled boats and caught with hand-thrown harpoons. In this dish, the fish is smothered under a thick cabbage soup.

Marinate the swordfish steak in the vinegar, 1 cup of the water, and rosemary for 1 hour.

In the meantime, break off and discard the outer leaves of the cabbage, core it, and cut it in ½-inch strips. Wash the strips and shake dry.

In a soup pot, sauté in the olive oil the garlic and the red pepper pods until browned. Remove and discard the garlic and pepper pods (or leave them in, if you wish). Add the cabbage strips and the salt (and cayenne pepper, if using). Cover, and simmer 20 to 25 minutes, stirring occasionally, until the cabbage has completely wilted. (Add a bit of water only if necessary.) When the cabbage is well cooked, add the wine, stir well, cook for another 1 to 2 minutes, and let rest.

While the cabbage is cooking: In a sauté pan large enough to accommodate the swordfish steak (cut in half, if necessary), combine the remaining 4 cups of water, the onion, celery, carrot, parsley. Bring to boil and simmer for 5 minutes. Add the swordfish, reduce the heat, and poach the fish at a simmer for 10 to 12 minutes. Remove the fish, reserving the cooking water, and cut the fish in large cubes.

(Cont.)

1 two-pound swordfish steak, about 1 inch thick

¼ cup wine vinegar

5 cups water

1 to 2 sprigs fresh rosemary, or 2 tablespoons dried

1 head Savoy cabbage (1½ to 2 pounds, approximate)

¼ cup olive oil

4 garlic cloves

2 to 3 red pepper pods, or 1 teaspoon powdered cayenne pepper

2 teaspoons salt

1 cup dry red wine

1 small onion, quartered

1 small celery rib

1 small carrot

1 sprig parsley

Italian-style bread, oven-warmed

Add salt and more cayenne pepper or Tabasco to taste. Divide the fish chunks among the serving dishes, and ladle the cabbage broth over them.

Serve with crusty Italian-style bread and a full-bodied red wine.

Sicilia

Rice, Asparagus, and Caciocavallo Cheese Soup
Minestra di riso, asparagi e caciocavallo

Lentil Soup with Pasta
Minestra di pasta e lenticchie

Puree of Fava Beans and Pasta Soup
Maccu siciliano

Maccu, Ragusa Style
Maccu ragusanu

Sicilian Fish Soup
Zuppa di pesce alla siciliana

Fish Stew with Couscous
Cuscusu co' a ghiotta 'e pisci

Sicilia

Sicily—where pine trees and palms, capers and cactus, passion flowers and a thousand other wildflowers grow—is a Garden of Eden. Greeks, Carthaginians, Romans, Arabs, Normans, Spaniards, and French thought so and were attracted to the tricornered island, making it their own, turning it into the veritable potpourri of cultures and ethnic traits it is today. Sicily is a sub-tropical land that hosts the snow-clad, fire-belching Mount Etna, soft sandy beaches and volcanic-black, knife-sharp coasts, sun-baked plains, green hills, and orange orchards, and above all, the sun—in winter, an orange gold-dripping sun; in summer, a white-hot, stone-blanching sun.

When we arrived, the mixed scents of sea, wildflowers, herbs, and orange blossoms enveloped us. We had a knowledgeable guide: writer, expert of all things Sicilian, gastronome, and poet. She spoke in romantic, poetic, declamatory turns of phrase; after a short time we too tended to speak as though on a Shakespearean stage.

Our travels started in Palermo, where the sacred and the profane meet—the city of Rosalia the Saint and of Roger II, fierce conqueror and king. Our guide drove us from one corner of town to the other; her driving was as florid as her speech, and as imaginative—even for Palermo. Her hands fluttered away from steering as if to trace in the air an ornate script: "Every stone of Palermo is history!"

And we saw Palermo, no stone unturned: a beautiful, bewildering city, changing its mood, its pace, its colors with the hours and light of day or night; a magic that touches the baroque churches, the Moorish palaces, the Norman castles, the grim alleys and the fragrant gardens, the stalls and the markets; and all scored by the music of noises and voices that plays from dawn well into the night. It is a voice that becomes deafening at the Ucciaria fish market. Every species of fish, shellfish, or mollusk that swims or crawls in Mediterranean waters is congregated on the metal-surfaced stalls here, their quality and prices hawked at full throat by the fishmongers.

"In the twelfth century," our guide yells to make herself heard, "an Arab described this market as sordid and fabulous, just like a pipe of hashish."

We moved west from Palermo, skirting the incredibly blue-green gulf of Castellammare, the town's fort dominating the miles-long, half-moon-shaped sandy beach, and then past the foothills of Corleone, on to Alcamo, and, flowering out of olive groves, the Greek Temple of Segesta.

Continuing west, once you reach Mount Erice high above Trapani, you have run out of Sicily. From the top of the mountain, all of Sicily is behind you. Below, at the edge of the sea, is Trapani, the city born from the sickle lost by Ceres while in search of her daughter Proserpina. "Trapani is where Arabia meets Sicily. To this tip came the Arabs; accustomed to the desert, they made of this land their enchanted garden, and with Oriental imagination enriched it."

As an afterthought to Sicily, a stone's throw west from Trapani and Mount Erice sprout the Isole Egadi, the Aegadian Isles: Favignana, Levanzo, and Maretimo. Or perhaps a Cyclops's throw: Interpreters of the *Odyssey* assert that Erice is the place from which Polyphemus, the Cyclops, pitched boulders at Ulysses, who then took shelter on the Isle of Goats, today's Favignana.

Tuna fishing has long since been the sustenance of this tiny archipelago. The big bluefin tuna pour through the Gibraltar Straits from the cold Atlantic into the Mediterranean and, on their way to spawn in warm Turkish waters, pass by the Aegadian Islands. It is here that they are slaughtered, and the islands make their life of tuna's death. Tuna, they say, is the sea equivalent of the pig: Nothing is wasted; each part has its use and value. If butchering tuna is an art, then the islanders are masters, with experience acquired by age: The very first representation of a tuna on record is on a rock wall graffito on the island of Maretimo. It dates back more than three thousand years, to neolithic times.

As for food, it is here that the Arabic couscous speaks Sicilian and blossoms into *cuscusu. Cuscusu co'a ghiotta 'e pisci:* couscous with a gluttony of fish!

We had met couscous years before, in North Africa—a tribal goat couscous, probably the very worst ever made, but our first and, Allah willing, our last. Allah, however, could do nothing against our mentor's rhapsodizing: "*Cuscusu* in Sicily is robed in legend. I will alert this little trattoria, and she will prepare it for you."

"She" was a beautifully enormous lady (we called her Juno), proprietress, cook, and waitress of a tiny eatery at the edge of the sea. She produced *cuscusu* for our enlightenment.

With saffron water and a few drops of olive oil she moistened a large shallow dish. With one hand she let semolina flour rain delicately on it, while the other hand pinched and glided through it, forming rice-sized grains. The two massive hands were engaged in such a delicate dance of their own that an odalisque could have learned a thousand secrets. . . . As the flour turned into couscous, she put it to rest on a board in the sun, gold bathed in gold and flavored with cinnamon, salt, pepper, and a few drops of olive oil, ready to be steamed.

"And now for the broth!" said Juno. And a broth she produced by putting in a mortar some garlic, almonds, parsley, cinnamon, and pepper and reducing all to a paste with a few powerful twists and blows of the pestle. She sautéed onions and to them added the paste and some tomato puree. Then she added, ever so slowly, warm water. "Now the broth has to boil," she said and, realizing our agony, added, "but only for a few minutes!" She smiled, and went on.

"For the *ghiotta* of fish, you need all kinds of fish, the more the better. And fresh!" she added. "They know when I make a *ghiotta,* and jump out of the water and come to me!" She laughed at the imagery, but we believed her.

Finally couscous and *ghiotta* came together: the golden, plump, moist couscous was a cradle for the stew of fish, and bathed in broth. Land and sea united, a living invocation of the Koran: "Nourish thyself, Oh believer, and rejoice in the generosity of Allah." We rejoiced and gratefully accepted the generosity: It changed forever our opinion of couscous.

Yes, at Trapani, Arabia meets Sicily, but it's an uneven match: When it comes to *cuscusu,* Sicily wins, hands down.

At Trapani, turn the bend of a Sicilian corner, head southeast, and you are on your way back toward Italy.

Agrigento follows, "called by the ancients the pearl of Magna Graecia, the most beautiful city, created not by gods but by mortal man."

Around Sicily's third corner comes Siracusa, "where the memory of Greece arrives with every wave of the Ionian Sea." And then Mount Etna, the largest live volcano in Europe, "regal in its ermine-white, snow-robed shoulders," and farther along is Taormina and its old Greek amphitheater, where "with the endless sea as background, all the human comedies and all the human tragedies could be played."

The intense blue of the coast is replaced inland by the gold of the wheat fields and the emerald green of the rolling hills, the explosions of color in the almond and cherry orchards, the lemon and orange groves, the shivering silver of the olive trees. Above all, a marvel of colors and tastes congregates on the Sicilian table: From a dish of pasta, tomato reds and eggplant purples wink from behind a chunk of white ricotta cheese; dark green capers dot the olive and artichoke greens of a casserole of vegetables; pink and rose and silver fish court the yellow of bell peppers in a soup; the sun-filtered reflections of a glass of garnet-red or golden wine dance on the white of a tablecloth. The whole astounding palette is displayed in the now soft, now violent colors of the famous *marzipani* sweets. If *cuscusu* is a gluttony of fish, the rest of Sicily's food challenges it with a gluttony of colors, flavors, and scents. Against the abundance of textures and colors, especially of the pasta dishes, soups compete with the sparkle and richness of their juices and broths.

And then Messina, first and last corner, our magic island's port of entry and of exit. Here we part—with a last flutter of hands—from our host, guide, and poet.

On the ferry taking us across the Straits of Messina, we watch Italy approach, with Scylla and Charybdis, now quiet monsters in their mythological Homeric recesses, letting us by unharmed.

Memories of this, and of previous trips, break through the surface of our minds like the dolphins piercing the sea in the ferry's wake. The island disappears behind the morning mist, and from the same ancient depths surfaces the memory of a poem:

> *Leaving you are now, but to return.*
> *If you don't wish to love me,*
> *Love me I will make you,*
> *Because by magic*
> *I make myself*
> *loved.*

Rice, Asparagus, and Caciocavallo Cheese Soup

Minestra di riso, asparagi e caciocavallo

Caciocavallo is a southern Italian cheese, recognized by its singular gourd shape. A raffia string ties two cheeses together by the neck so they can straddle a pole and be hung to dry. Provolone cheese is very similar to caciocavallo but for the shape; it is also more easily found in American markets, and it makes a good substitute.

Cut the asparagus in 1½-inch lengths and cook in 2½ quarts lightly salted water for about 5 minutes, or until cooked but still very firm. Scoop it out, set aside, and keep warm. Reserve the cooking water.

In a large soup pot, sauté the minced onion, garlic, parsley, and the sliced bacon in the olive oil until the mince is golden and the bacon strips are limp but not crisp. Add approximately 8 cups of the asparagus cooking water, bring to a boil, and add the rice. Stir, reduce the heat, and cook about 12 minutes. Stir in the asparagus and cook another 2 to 3 minutes, or until the rice is tender.

Remove the pot from the heat, and add the cubed cheese. Mix and serve immediately before the cheese melts completely.

1½ pounds asparagus, cleaned and trimmed

1 small onion, minced

1 garlic clove, minced

2 tablespoons minced flat-leaf parsley

3 ounces lean bacon, cut in thin strips

¼ cup olive oil

¾ cup long-grain rice

5 ounces caciocavallo or sharp provolone, cubed

Lentil Soup with Pasta

Minestra di pasta e lenticchie

1 pound dried lentils

2 small onions

1 celery rib

2 teaspoons salt

4 ounces pancetta or lean salt pork

2 garlic cloves

4 to 5 tablespoons chopped flat-leaf parsley

4 tablespoons olive oil

2 cups canned plum tomatoes, chopped

Freshly ground pepper

10 ounces perciatelli or thin macaroni

Grated pecorino Romano cheese

Soak the lentils in enough cold water to cover, for at least 2 hours. Drain and put them in a soup pot with 3 quarts of cold water, 1 of the onions, the celery rib, and the salt. Bring to a boil, reduce the heat, and simmer, covered, for about 25 minutes, or until the lentils are tender. Drain and reserve the cooking water.

Mince together the pancetta, garlic, the remaining onion, and 2 tablespoons of the parsley. In a large soup pot, sauté the mince in the olive oil until the mince is golden. Add the chopped tomatoes, and cook at a low boil for 5 minutes, or until the sauce has reduced a bit. Add the drained lentils, stir, and cook 2 to 3 minutes. Add 8 cups of the reserved cooking water (add warm water if necessary) and bring to a boil.

With your hands, break the pasta into 2-inch lengths and add to the boiling pot. Cook 8 to 10 minutes, or until the pasta is tender. Remove from the heat. Let the soup sit for 1 to 2 minutes, then serve topped with the remaining parsley and the grated pecorino Romano cheese.

Puree of Fava Beans and Pasta Soup

Maccu siciliano

Maccu in Sicilian dialect means "bruised" or, in culinary terms, pureed—referring specifically to fava.

Soak the dried fava beans in enough cold water to cover for at least 24 hours. Drain. Place the fava beans in a large saucepan with enough lightly salted cold water to cover (about 1½ quarts, but depending on the quality of the beans, you may need to add more during cooking). Bring to a boil, reduce the heat, cover, and simmer for 30 minutes.

In a skillet, sauté the minced onion and garlic, the salt pork strips, and the cayenne pepper in the olive oil until the mince is golden and limp. Add the sautéed mince to the half-cooked fava beans, and stir. Cook for another 30 minutes, or until the beans are very soft.

Drain the beans, and reserve the cooking water. Pass the beans through a food mill or a food processor, forming a puree. (It should be smooth, reasonably creamy, and batter-like.) Add the reserved cooking water as needed to achieve the right consistency. Return the puree to the saucepan and keep warm.

In a second pot, cook the pasta in lightly salted boiling water for 8 to 10 minutes. Drain well, and add the pasta to the puree. Stir and cook over medium heat for 1 to 2 minutes. If the soup is too thick, add a bit more of the reserved cooking water.

Serve hot or at room temperature, topped with a sprinkle of grated pecorino Romano cheese.

1½ pounds dried fava beans

Salt

1 onion, minced

2 garlic cloves, minced

4 ounces lean salt pork or bacon, cut in thin strips

½ teaspoon powdered cayenne pepper

¼ cup olive oil

10 ounces small cut pasta, such as ditalini, cannolicchi, or elbows

Freshly grated pecorino Romano cheese

Maccu, Ragusa Style

Maccu ragusanu

The town of Ragusa produces a colorful variation on *Maccu* by adding vegetable greens and shredded cheese, thus becoming *Maccu ragusanu.*

1 *recipe* Maccu siciliano *(page 223) with or without pasta*

1½ pounds (approximate) Swiss chard, or 1 head romaine lettuce

Shredded pecorino Romano cheese

Prepare the *Maccu siciliano* as directed.

Trim and wash the Swiss chard. Cut the greens in 2-inch lengths, separating the white stem from the leafy green. Add the white parts to a pot of lightly salted boiling water, and when the pot returns to a boil, add the leafy parts. Cook just until done (about 3 to 5 minutes), and drain. Mix with the prepared *maccu,* or serve half greens alongside half *maccu* on each serving dish. Serve warm or at room temperature, sprinkled with shredded pecorino Romano cheese.

Sicilian Fish Soup

Zuppa di pesce alla siciliana

The particularity of this dish is that the fish is baked/steamed in a sealed casserole and produces its own broth. The whole work is in the assembly—the fish and the oven do the rest. For best results, avoid oily fish, such as mackerel or bluefish, or very delicately fleshed fish, such as sole or flounder.

Preheat the oven to 350°F.

Clean and scale the fish without removing the heads and tails, if possible. Cut the fish into chunks and place them in a large ovenproof casserole with a tight-fitting cover.

Arrange the shrimp, shells on, on top of the fish. Clean and cut up the squid, and arrange the pieces atop the shrimp. Scrub and debarb the mussels, and add to the casserole.

Cut the onion into thin slivers, and add them along with the minced parsley and black olives to the casserole. Add the garlic, peppercorns, and red pepper pods, if using, and sink the bay leaf into the middle of everything. Add the olive oil, and tip the casserole gently back and forth to distribute the oil. Sprinkle with the salt and add the wine.

Cut a round of brown wrapping paper just a little larger than the casserole, and place it between the cover and the casserole to seal in the vapors while cooking. Bake for 30 minutes.

While the casserole bakes, barely moisten the bread slices with a bit of olive oil and oven-toast them to a golden brown. Arrange the toasts in the serving dishes, with *zuppa di pesce* ladled over. Serve immediately.

6 to 7 varieties fresh fish (about 5½ to 6 pounds, before cleaning), such as 1 to 2 small porgies, 1 whiting, 1 snapper, 1 small monkfish steak, ½ pound shrimp, ½ pound squid, 1 pound mussels

1 onion

¼ cup minced Italian flat-leaf parsley

1 cup Sicilian or Greek black olives, pitted

2 garlic cloves

5 peppercorns

2 red pepper pods, or a dash of Tabasco (optional)

1 bay leaf

½ cup olive oil, plus more as needed

2 teaspoons salt

1½ cups very dry white wine

6 to 12 slices Italian-style bread

Fish Stew with Couscous

Cuscusu co' a ghiotta 'e pisci

For this fish stew choose any combination of fresh fish the market has to offer, but avoid oily fish, such as mackerel or bluefish, and delicately fleshed fish, such as sole or flounder.

FOR THE BROTH:

1 medium onion, finely chopped

2 garlic cloves, minced

½ cup blanched almonds, coarsely chopped

2 tablespoons minced fresh flat-leaf parsley

½ teaspoon powdered cayenne pepper

¼ cup olive oil

½ cup dry white wine

2 cups canned Italian peeled tomatoes, drained and chopped

2 teaspoons salt

4 pounds fish heads, bones, and tails

½ pound medium shrimp, shelled and deveined, with shells reserved

FOR THE COUSCOUS:

1 tablespoon olive oil

¼ teaspoon cinnamon

¼ teaspoon salt

Mince together the onion, garlic, almonds, parsley, and cayenne and process to a coarse paste, using a food processor if possible.

In a soup pot over medium heat, sauté the paste in the olive oil and cook until golden, about 5 minutes.

Stir in the wine and cook until the liquid has reduced by half. Add the tomatoes and cook over high heat for 2 to 3 minutes, breaking up the tomatoes with a wooden spoon. Add 4 cups of water, and bring the mixture to a boil. Add the fish heads, bones, and tails, and the reserved shrimp shells. Return the pot to boil, cover, and simmer for 30 minutes. Remove from the heat and allow to cool a bit. Using a fine sieve or a colander lined with cheesecloth, strain the broth into a second soup pot. Bring the strained broth to a boil over high heat and cook until it has reduced to about 4 cups.

Rinse the first soup pot and in it bring to a boil 1 cup of the fish broth, 1½ cups of water, the olive oil, cinnamon, salt, and saffron. Stir in the couscous, and as soon as the pot returns to a boil, remove from the heat. Cover and let stand for 5 minutes.

Bring the remaining 3 cups of broth to a boil. Add the mussels, cover, and cook until they open, about 4 minutes. Scoop them out and transfer to a platter.

Add the firmest fish to the broth; cover and simmer for about 4 minutes. Transfer the cooked fish to the platter with the mussels. Add the more delicate fish and the shrimp to the broth and simmer until the fish is cooked and the shrimp turn pink, about 2 to 3 minutes. Transfer them also to the platter.

To serve, fluff the couscous and arrange in a ring in each of the serving dishes. Spoon the fish, shrimp, and mussels inside the couscous ring and ladle the remaining hot broth over all.

¼ teaspoon saffron powder or crushed saffron threads

1½ cups couscous

FOR THE FISH:

½ pound mussels, scrubbed and debarded

3½ pounds assorted filets of firm-fleshed fish (such as grouper, monkfish, halibut, snapper, whiting) cut in 2-inch pieces

Sardegna

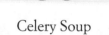

Celery Soup
Minestra di sedano

Sardinian Couscous Soup
Fregula o succu

Tomato and Fregula Soup
Minestra di fregula al pomodoro

Music-Paper Soup
Pane frattau

Vegetable, Meatball, and Fregula Soup
Cascà

Sardegna

G eologically, Sardinia's soil is some of the oldest in Europe. Together with Val d'Aosta and Trentino in the Alps, the island emerged from the sea while the rest of Italy and most of the continent were still making bubbles underwater, submerged for a few more eons. Sardinia is an island, isolated in early time but also in space: It is more distant from other continental lands than any other country in the Mediterranean. Perhaps for this reason, and for the fact that the mostly rough and mountainous land does not offer many easy landfalls, Sardinia was the last to be inhabited by Neanderthal man. It suffered a chronological delay: Anthropological and historical ages came late and out of phase to this island.

Sardinia is at the crossroad of all the sea traffic of the Mediterranean; after Sicily, it is that sea's second largest island. From prehistory to modern times, its strategic position and its considerable mineral resources made it particularly appealing. Large finds of obsidian (the vitreous rock from which prehistory's sharpest cutting and scraping tools were made) and then abundant deposits of copper and lead, zinc and silver, tin and iron, attracted foreign colonizers/predators to the island. Cretans, Phoenicians, Carthaginians, Greeks, Etruscans, Romans, Vandals, Pisans, Genoese, and Spaniards all gave birth to particular immigrant cultures, continually evolving and at the same time perennially insular and peculiarly Sardinian. The various colonizers created economic peaks, alternated by periods of abandonment and desertion, instilling in the Sardinians a strong sense of resiliency and self-containment—"I bend but I don't break!"

Later in time, the frequent raids from the sea drove the sparse inhabitants to the rough mountains of the interior, fracturing the population into small independent communities of hunter/shepherds, who were fiercely jealous of their turf and frequently warring with one another. This migration produced a race of anomalous islanders, a people dedicated more to the land and the flock than to the sea. Taciturn, tall, straight, and strong, their character and appearance are matched by the famous beauty of the Sardinian women, deserving models for the ancient Sardinian deity "Great Mother," the worshiped Mother Earth. All traits that, while contributing to shape an upright, inflexibly proud race, also fostered a slower sociopolitical development.

Many of the "colonizers" elected to spend the gains squeezed out of Sardinia on other lands, letting the islanders fend for themselves. The pattern lasted well into the 1800s and provoked frequent resentment and rebellion against the governments in power, resulting in widely practiced and brutal banditry.

Throughout history, the timeless and abundant natural beauty of the island was overlooked, and Sardinia was known best as a place of exile and punishment. Today the whole island is fast catching up and is now governed as an autonomous region—it can finally use its agricultural and mineral resources to its own advantage.

Its two major cities, Sassari and Cagliari, are located at the very north and south of the island. In the south, in the center of the gulf by the same name, Cagliari is a modern sprawling city and Sardinia's capital. It overlooks its sparkling blue bay, the nearby lagoon, and the evergreen pinewoods; the view is closed at the near horizon by the bleached white strip of the sea-salt beds, a major supplier of salt to Italy. The active port, bustling since Carthaginian times, is one of the island's primary links to the continent. The city treasures memories of Greek, Roman, Pisan, and Spanish influences in its well-preserved amphitheater, public buildings, and churches.

Sassari is the second largest Sardinian city. In the early 1800s, Carlo Felice of Savoy, king of Piedmont and Sardinia, built the road that crosses the entire island, connecting Sassari with Cagliari, as a means to Sardinian progress—progress that took nearly 150 years to arrive.

Today a major highway follows the traces of the old road, carrying most of the traffic between south and north. It heads northwest to reach the west coast at Oristano, capital of one of the four provinces, and there it splits: one branch continues north to Sassari and the other west to touch Nuoro in the mountains and then Olbia and its splendid gulf on the east coast. Many neolithic tombs and temples pepper the island, and so do the many startling *nuraghi*—unique, massive cylindrical towers constructed without mortar with huge, city bus–size stones, sometimes surrounded by small villages of similar construction. Legend says that Daedalus, fleeing from Minos's Crete, took refuge in Sardinia and, as compensation for the natives' hospitality, taught them how to build the *nuraghi*. Today they are the most tangible, unforgettable remains of the Nuragic civilization, which flourished from about 1600 to 100 B.C. and was a major event in Sardinia's cultural past.

The pristine beauty of the rocky coastline, the hundreds of coves and inlets and their crystal-clear azure waters, have spurred local and foreign investment to develop sea resorts, including the world-famous, spectacularly luxurious Costa Smeralda.

Each of the many Sardinian provinces, cities, and villages has proudly retained its local cuisine; all are based, naturally, on tradition and on the main local supplies and economies. Fish are everywhere, lobster chiefly in the northern coasts; beef and dairy command the table of the southwestern plain of the Campidano; lamb and baby goat meat and sheep cheeses (famous among them the pecorino *sardo*) enrich the central regions. Some still show old foreign influences, such as the soups with *fregula,* a direct recall of the North African couscous.

And just as varied are the Sardinian wines. So wide is their production that the island could be thought of as a vineyard floating on the sea, its roots reaching into history. The Sardinian art of winemaking is very old, but the quality of the wines is of recent fame. Sardinian wines were considered so poor by ancient Romans that they had a good trade going: the jars the Romans brought to Sardinia full of good Roman wine returned to Rome full of silver. Today the process is reversed: Excellent Sardinian Cannonau, Malvasia, Nuragus, Vermentino, Vernaccia, Moscato flow freely and widely abroad and are a connoisseur's find.

The wines are a perfect match for the food, which is simple and flavorful. Sea breezes carry the ancient aromas of wild herbs and enrich that of venison, wild boar, fish, baby goat, lamb, and cheeses grilled on wood fires.

All is accompanied by the uniquely Sardinian *carta da musica.* Probably of Middle Eastern origin, it is a bread as thin as a page of musical score, singed in spots by the griddle, originally produced as sustenance for shepherds, who could carry it forever without its spoiling.

Old wine, traditional food, ageless bread: a mirror, perhaps, of the unspoiled, most beautifully varied, timeless land of Sardinia.

Celery Soup

Minestra di sedano

1 celery bunch

2 garlic cloves, minced

1 onion, minced

1 carrot, minced

2 to 3 sprigs flat-leaf parsley, minced

4 tablespoons olive oil

10 ounces lean beef, ground or cut in tiny cubes

½ teaspoon salt

½ cup dry red wine

2 tablespoons flour

6 ounces music-paper bread (page 264), or as needed

Grated pecorino Romano cheese

Clean and trim the celery, and cut the ribs into 2-inch lengths. Boil the celery in 8 cups of lightly salted water for 10 minutes. Scoop out the cooked celery, set aside, and reserve the cooking water.

In a soup pot over medium heat, sauté the minced garlic, onion, carrot, and parsley in the olive oil until the mince is golden and limp. Increase the heat, add the beef, and cook for 5 minutes. Add the wine and stir, cooking until the wine has nearly evaporated. Add the flour, stir until well mixed, and cook another 2 to 3 minutes.

Add the reserved cooking water, and bring the mixture to a low boil.

Cut the cooked celery pieces into thin sticks and add to the soup pot. Simmer until the celery is completely cooked, about 10 minutes.

Line each serving dish with *carta da musica,* ladle the soup over it, and serve with a generous sprinkling of grated pecorino Romano cheese.

Sardinian Couscous Soup

Fregula o succu

Fregula is the Sardinian equivalent of the Sicilian *cuscusu* but with slightly larger grains, closer in size to a peppercorn rather than a rice grain.

Combine the flour and salt. Dissolve the saffron in the water. Moisten a large shallow plate with some saffron water, and dust the plate generously with the flour mixture. Rub and pinch the tips of your fingers over the flour in a rotary motion: the flour will turn into little round lumps or grains. A little experience will suggest the right flour/water proportion for obtaining the peppercorn sizes. Allow the *fregula* to dry on kitchen towels or cookie sheets. Place the dried grains in a colander, and shake: the small grains will fall through. (Use these to thicken other soups.)

In a soup pot over medium heat, bring the broth to a boil, then stir into it the *fregula*. Cook 4 to 5 minutes (more or less, depending on the dryness of the fregula). Serve with a large sprinkling of grated pecorino *sardo* cheese.

12 ounces coarse-grained semolina flour

¼ teaspoon salt

⅛ teaspoon powdered saffron

¼ cup lukewarm water

8 cups beef broth

Freshly grated pecorino sardo *(sharp) cheese*

Tomato and Fregula Soup

Minestra di fregula al pomodoro

1 small onion, minced

2 garlic cloves, minced

1 celery rib, minced

4 tablespoons flat-leaf Italian parsley, minced

1 teaspoon salt

Dash of freshly ground pepper

¼ cup olive oil

4 cups crushed peeled plum tomatoes, fresh or canned

6 cups chicken broth

10 ounces fregula (*see previous recipe*)

6 to 7 fresh basil leaves, chopped

Freshly grated pecorino cheese

In a large saucepan over medium heat, sauté the minced onion, garlic, celery, parsley, salt, and pepper in the olive oil. When the mince is limp and golden, stir in the crushed tomatoes.

Bring the mixture to a boil and simmer for 15 to 20 minutes, or until the sauce has thickened. Allow to cool. Pass the sauce through a sieve or a food mill into a soup pot. Add the broth, and bring to a boil. Stir in the *fregula,* and cook for 5 minutes, or until the *fregula* is tender.

Serve warm, topped with the basil and grated pecorino cheese.

Note: For a reasonable shortcut, dilute 4 cups of tomato or vegetable juice, such as V8, with 4 cups of broth and cook the *fregula* in it.

Music-Paper Soup

Pane frattau

Sardinia, perhaps more than any other Italian region, has a mystic attachment to bread. Nearly every town and village has its own bread, as well as special breads for every occasion, sacred or profane. Regionally, *carta da musica* bread represents them all. In this simple *pane frattau* soup, it serves as base and holds together all the other nutritional elements of the dish.

Place 4 cups of the broth in a saucepan, and the remaining 4 cups in a sauté pan. Bring both pans to a low boil.

Arrange large chips (about 3 × 5 inches) of music-paper bread or pita bread separated into layers among individual serving dishes. Spread tomato sauce over them.

In the boiling broth in the sauté pan, poach the eggs. Transfer the eggs with a slotted spoon to the bread topped with the tomato sauce.

Chop or shred the basil leaves and divide among the serving dishes, sprinkled atop the poached eggs. Add a generous sprinkle of the shredded pecorino.

Ladle hot broth from the saucepan over all. Serve hot.

8 cups beef broth

6 ounces music-paper bread (page 264) or pita bread

1½ cups tomato sauce

6 large eggs

9 to 10 fresh basil leaves

Shredded pecorino sardo *(sharp) cheese*

Vegetable, Meatball, and Fregula Soup

Cascà

10 ounces ground beef, or a mix of beef and veal

1 large egg

1 tablespoon unflavored bread crumbs

2 tablespoons minced flat-leaf Italian parsley

2 teaspoons salt

1 head cauliflower (approximately 1 pound when cored and trimmed)

10 ounces fresh peas or frozen baby peas, thawed

3 tablespoons olive oil

2 to 3 whole cloves

1 to 2 tablespoons lemon juice

8 ounces fregula (page 235)

Freshly grated pecorino cheese

In a mixing bowl, combine the ground meat with the egg, bread crumbs, parsley, and a pinch of the salt. Shape into walnut-size meatballs, and set them aside to dry out a bit.

In a soup pot, bring 2 quarts of lightly salted water to a boil.

Core the cauliflower and separate it into flowerets. Add the flowerets, peas, olive oil, and cloves to the soup pot. Reduce the heat and simmer for 5 minutes. Increase the heat, bring to a low boil, add the meatballs and the lemon juice, and cook another 5 minutes. Add the *fregula* and cook another 5 minutes, or until the *fregula* is tender. Remove from the heat, and allow to rest for a few minutes. Serve with grated pecorino cheese.

Basics

Equipment

Ingredients

Broth
Beef Broth
Chicken Broth
Vegetable Broth
Fish Broth

Pasta
Homemade Pasta
Food-Processor Pasta Dough
Handmade Pasta Dough
Apulian Homemade Pasta

Bread
White Bread
Whole Wheat Bread
Sardinian Music-Paper Bread

Equipment

FOOD MILL   A food mill incorporates the advantages of a sieve with those of a vegetable grater/grinder. The hand-rotated paddles push the vegetables through the changeable, different-sized perforated disks at the bottom of the mill. While the liquid part passes through freely, the solids are coarsely grated or pureed and collected in the vessel on which the mill rests. The unwanted parts (seeds, peels, skins, etc.) remain in the mill.

PASTA POT   As the name says, this is a pot for boiling pasta. What makes it different is the removable colander that lines the pot. This pot also comes in handy when making broths: At the end of cooking, the colander is lifted out, along with the solids that went to make the broth. It saves the sometimes messy operation of pouring the contents of one pot through a sieve and into another pot or container.

PRESSURE COOKER   This pot is an excellent tool for cutting cooking time, especially where soups with meats or long-cooking ingredients are involved. (The best advice on using it is given in the instructions that come with the cooker, adjusted by personal experience.) Under its sealed cover, a pressure cooker holds all the ingredients' nutrients. But somehow it takes away some of the mystique of a soup pot bubbling away on the stove and warming up the kitchen. . . .

SIEVE   A sieve is used in the final stages of broth making. Fine-meshed and lined with *cheesecloth,* a sieve will retain any unwanted particles when used to strain a broth.

SKIMMER   As the name implies, a skimmer is a large, round sieve spoon designed to skim off the undesired matter that bubbles to the surface of a broth, either at rest or while cooking.

SLOTTED SPOON   This utensil is a large cooking spoon with slots or holes, made to scoop solids out of liquids. In a pinch, it can do the work of a skimmer, but not as well.

SOUP POT   A soup pot comes in different sizes, measured in quarts. It should be made of good heat-retaining metal, such as copper or thick aluminum, and it should have a tight-fitting cover. It is a tall pot, about two times as tall as its diameter: By the convection principle (heat rises, cold descends), a simmering liquid stirs itself gently as it bubbles along and gives a better flavor exchange among its ingredients.

Ingredients

~

The best ingredients make the best soup, but what counts is the spirit of the old Roman saying: "*Tutto fà brodo!*" or, metaphorically, "In a pinch, everything goes!" Similar ingredients can be added or substituted or even left out, if the spirit is respected. For example, at times we have used savoy cabbage instead of purple cabbage without injury—and without the Gourmet Police coming after us.

BEANS   Fresh, dried, or canned, beans are a main ingredient in Italian soups. There are literally hundreds of bean varieties, but Italian cuisine takes advantage of only half a dozen at most. Dried beans allow for easy storage, and the still-used procedure of soaking overnight before cooking has been updated and hastened by the pressure cooker. One thing to keep in mind is that 1 cup of dried beans becomes 2 cups when soaked and cooked. Fastest of all—and quite frankly, just as good if not better—is using canned beans. Just make sure that they are packaged with only the addition of salt and no sweeteners or other flavors. When making soup with canned beans, add the canning water for flavor and thickness. For salads and other purposes, drain and rinse the beans.

BREAD   Italian-style, fresh from the oven, or old and dried out; pristine or in saved leftovers; cut in slices and toasted or fried in butter or oil; white made with unbleached flour, or whole wheat dark: Bread is an essential part of Italian *zuppa*. The number of slices per serving is a matter of personal choice and determined by the size of the bread. Regional breads—and there are hundreds—vary in diameter from that of a cartwheel to a shepherd's stock, thus a slice of one is quite different from another. Most of the time, the bread slices (about ½ an inch thick) go *into* the soup plate and should barely cover its bottom. Then the soup is ladled over the bread. For homemade bread recipes, see pages 261–265.

BROTH   Anything boiled in water makes broth. To make good broth, see pages 250–255.

BUTTER   In the Italian kitchen, butter is unsalted, which gives more control of the saltiness of any dish.

CAPON or FOWL   These terms are the commercial labels for larger or older chickens, which are considered perfect for making excellent broth. Do not pass them up if you find them on the market.

CHICKPEAS   For the Italian *ceci,* or chickpeas, follow same advice as for beans, page 243.

FAVA FRESCA   Fresh fava beans show up in the spring in six- to twelve-inch-long green pods. Shell them to get at the seeds, the edible part inside. The seeds themselves have an outer, edible skin (which may be removed quite easily) around the seed proper. Choose the medium-size, softer pods; the seeds of the very big or very hard pods must be peeled and do not have as gentle a flavor as the smaller ones. Cook them in lightly salted boiling water, simmering for about 30 minutes, depending on size.

FAVA SECCA   Dried fava beans, which can be found in Italian or Mideastern specialty stores, must be soaked for about 24 hours before cooking. They should be cooked starting with cold, lightly salted water brought to a boil and then simmered for 1 or 1½ hours. Depending on quality, the bean skins could resist cooking and remain somewhat tough, in which case they should be cooked longer, or the skins may be removed altogether.

HERBS AND SPICES   An important part of soup making, herbs and spices are frequently used fresh, but the dried version may be substituted when necessary. Both herbs and spices are like friends—too many present at one time can be overwhelming. Also, since no two palates are the same, start with a little bit—it may go a long way. Our use of herbs and spices in all the recipes is our average dose, the middle ground. Here is a brief description of those most frequently called for in Italy's soups:

Basil   An annual herb with a sweet odor, basil has a superior taste when it is at its freshest. Basil leaves, if purchased in bunches, may be held with their stems in water until used or, without stems, in olive oil. Also, the leaves may be frozen in water in ice cube trays. Basil leaves, in an emergency, may be used dried. (They taste fine for up to three months.) Basil is used in salads, sauces, stews, and soups.

Bay or Laurel Leaves   Bay leaves have been used as an herb for hundreds of years. Those most frequently found on the American market are from California, carefully dried to preserve flavor and color. When using in soups for the first time, begin with half a leaf to make sure the flavor is pleasing to your taste. Bay leaves are also used in other home-style cookery, such as marinades for fish and meat. Discard bay leaves before serving.

Chives   A perennial plant, chives have long grasslike leaves with an oniony flavor and round lavender flowers. If you grow the plant yourself, pick only as needed: The plant keeps producing all summer long. Generally chives are used minced as a final savory addition to a soup, and are also added to cheese, potatoes, and eggs.

Cloves   The spicy dried buds of a tropical tree, and a member of the myrtle family, cloves are used as a spice. They convey a sweet-smelling perk to many a soup.

Garlic   A plant of the onion family, garlic is used in Italian cookery far less than many people think. It has a round bulb with many sections, called cloves, and in most recipes, one or two cloves are deemed enough. Frequently garlic cloves are browned in olive oil to flavor it, then removed and discarded.

Marjoram and Oregano   Both pungent, aromatic herbs, marjoram and oregano are close cousins, so to speak. Sweet marjoram is a half-hardy perennial grown as an annual in cold climates. It may be used fresh, snipping off its small, oval, velvety leaves as needed. It may also be dried, harvested just before flowering and hung in small, loosely tied bunches. Oregano, a spreading hardy perennial, is also known as pot marjoram. It has abundant large and shiny leaves and a more zesty taste than sweet marjoram. It is commonly used dried since it fully conserves its aroma.

Parsley   A biennial herb, parsley is usually grown as an annual. Of its two varieties, curly-leaf and flat-leaf, the latter is considered ordinary parsley in Italian cookery. It has a stronger flavor and aroma than its curly-leaf cousin, which is used more as a garnish than a flavor.

Rosemary   An evergreen perennial herb that can grow up to five feet in height, rosemary smells like pine needles when it is crushed. In cold climates, it is grown indoors and, space allowing, can carry on for years. In addition to its use in soups, rosemary is grand when tucked under the skin of a roasting chicken or chicken pieces in grilling and broiling.

Sage   A perennial Mediterranean herb, sage may stay in the garden all year long, even in cold climates. A member of the mint family, it has silvery-green, softly textured (almost fuzzy) leaves, vaguely bitter but with a lovely fragrance. Sage cuttings may be hung to dry if not bunched together too tightly.

Tarragon   A bushy perennial herb with narrow, pointed leaves, tarragon has a sweet aroma and flavor. While best when used fresh, tarragon leaves may be stored in vinegar and removed as desired. Tarragon is fine with fish, tomatoes, and eggs as well as in soups.

Thyme   A tiny-leafed, wide-spreading perennial, thyme has many varieties. The two most frequently found on the American market are the narrow-leaf French thyme, with its gray-green balsamic foliage, and a second variety with glistening, strongly lemon-scented leaves. In addition to its use in soups, thyme is also a good addition to marinades.

HOT PEPPER or RED PEPPER POD   Also known as cayenne or *peperoncino rosso,* hot pepper pods are frequently used, fresh or dried, to flavor and to spike up the overall taste of food. When dried, the pepper pod is seeded and sautéed in olive oil to flavor it, and removed and discarded when its color has gone from a warm red to a very dark brown. Tabasco sauce may serve as a substitute, but *peperoncino* gives a purer flavor, as it is not mixed with vinegar; on the other hand, *peperoncino* may vary in "hotness," which can be controlled by tasting and varying the cooking times, while Tabasco spiciness is constant. Powdered cayenne pepper may be used instead of the pod. It loses some of its "hotness" with time, so it is advisable to check its age by purchase date.

OLIVE OIL   Used more often than butter in the Italian cuisine, olive oil is available labeled "pure olive oil," "virgin olive oil," and "extra-virgin olive oil." We consider the first lighter and with a less definite taste, the second better for general cooking use, and the latter the perfect condiment and final garnish for a soup.

PANCETTA   An alternative for *lean salt pork,* pancetta is available in Italian specialty markets. It is lean salt pork tightly rolled and salted. Sometimes it comes highly spiced, in which case some of the spices (mostly coarse ground pepper) should be scraped away.

PASTA   It is a one-word culinary universe, well worth exploring. As a first step, the existence of two major galaxies should be recognized: commercial pasta (dry pasta) and homemade pasta (fresh pasta or *pasta all'uovo*). In many places, you can now buy commercial fresh pasta. It is wrong to think that one is better than the other; each has its own character, merit, and uses.

Commercial pasta or "dry pasta" is made by mixing wheat flour (semolina) and water and extruding the resulting dough through different-size dies and then drying it; it has a very long shelf life.

Homemade pasta or *pasta all'uovo* (egg pasta) is made by mixing all-purpose unbleached flour with eggs and rolling the resulting dough; the pasta should be used immediately, or before it dries out.

When it comes to soups, commercial pasta supplies an infinity of small shapes—farfalle, farfalline, tubetti, tubettini, orzo, stelline, acini, capelli d'angelo, capellini—enough to make a libretto for an opera. The recipes here will often give the American name, such as "small elbows," even if less romantic.

For *homemade pasta* and how to make it, see pages 256–260.

PORCINI MUSHROOMS   Imported from Italy and available in many specialty shops and supermarkets, porcini are wild mushrooms that grow in spring and fall in the moist shade of mountain woods. Either very fresh or dried, they are a connoisseur's delight. Nobody has been able to grow them commercially, so they are reasonably expensive. Sometimes they are available fresh in American specialty markets but, even if flown in, usually they are past their prime and hardly worth the expense or effort. The dried porcini lack the bulk and texture of the fresh but pack all the aroma and flavor, which they efficiently pass on to more humble mushrooms when cooked together. A few porcini do the trick. Before using, they should be soaked in warm water for 15 to 20 minutes. The soaking water, properly strained, may be used to flavor the soup.

PORK RIND   Often appearing with a different name in many Italian regions, the most common being *cotenna* or *cotica,* pork rind is pork skin with all the fat removed. (If not, it is easy to scrape the fat away, or ask the butcher to do it for you.) It seems to have universal appeal in all peasant cuisines, especially when associated with beans. Its gelatin content thickens a dish and gives it a particularly pleasing consistency, if used judiciously. Pork rind is not for everyone, but once in the dish, it can easily be removed and set aside for *cotenna* lovers to pounce on.

PORTABELLA   Large farm-grown mushrooms, portabella are the size and color of fresh porcini mushrooms but unfortunately lack their taste and especially their aroma. They are good to use with the dried porcini when size and texture are important.

RICE   Italy grows and markets several major types of rice, among them arborio, carnaroli, and vialone, all three of which are short- to medium-grain and will cook up well in almost any dish. Rice should not be rinsed: The water will wash away some of the starch that gives creaminess to a soup or a risotto, for which these rices are special. These varieties of rice may be found in many food and specialty stores in the United States. However, Texas also grows a fine medium-grain variety, called River Rice, packaged by Riviana.

SALT PORK, LEAN   Salt pork is salted, unsmoked bacon. It should come striped equally by lean meat and fat; otherwise, choose the leanest and trim some of the fat away. Its rind should be removed. In the great majority of its uses, it is minced with other flavorings as a base for soups or sauces. It comes in different degrees of saltiness, depending on the brand. As it is used in relatively small quantities, its saltiness goes to flavor the soup. If too salty (only you can decide) the salt pork may be blanched for a minute or two in boiling water. Generally, one slice of salt pork measures 5 to 6 inches long, 1 inch wide, and ⅛ inch thick and is about 1 to 1½ ounces in weight. Lean bacon or slab bacon are adequate substitutes in flavoring soups.

SQUID   Squid appears frequently in Italian fish soups. One Italian variety, called *calamari* or cuttlefish, is slender and favors the Italian west coast; another, *seppia,* is plumper and favors the east coast. The two are biologically related, and their differences do not show once in the soup. They are available fresh or frozen, and most of the time they have to be cleaned by the buyer. Cleaning squid is a simple procedure:

- Remove the tentacles by cutting between them and the eyes.
- With your fingers, pop out the bony mouth at the base of the tentacles.
- Reserve the tentacles. Hold the squid under a gentle stream of running water.
- While squeezing the body (mantle) like a toothpaste tube, pull away at the head, which will come out with the attached innards. Discard.
- Pull out and discard the translucent, flexible quill-like bone (the cuttlefish has a white, thicker one).
- Peel off the mantle's thin reddish outer membrane, and rinse the body, now resembling an empty tube, in and out.
- Cut into ½ to ¾-inch-wide rings, and cook as directed.

TOMATO, PLUM   This tomato variety is grown in Italy especially for use in sauces. It is essential that fresh plum tomatoes are perfectly ripe; if not, it will be impossible to get any sauce out of them. Some strains have been developed to withstand the rigors of travel from faraway places and are permanently hard and uncookable (they also lack aroma and flavor), hence much better the use of canned plum tomatoes, domestic or imported. Of these, the reputed best are the San Marzano plum tomatoes, grown in the Campania region. The canned tomatoes are available "whole," "crushed," "kitchen ready," and "pureed." They all do the same job, but whole are preferable if some final texture is desirable.

TOMATO PASTE   Tomato paste is also called tomato concentrate, because that's what it is—a thick paste made by boiling down the sieved pulp of fresh tomatoes, with no other flavors added. A little goes a long way, and it is generally diluted (1 heaping tablespoon per cup of warm water) before using. In soups, it is mostly used as a spike or for adding a blush of color to an otherwise bland or pale soup. Once the can is opened, the remaining paste in the can tends to oxidize: Transfer the paste to a plastic container, and cover the surface with plastic wrap. Tomato paste in smaller quantity comes also in tubes, which avoids the oxidation problem.

TOMATO SAUCE   The basic sauce—and the base for more complex creations—tomato sauce is made with ripe plum tomatoes and flavored with carrots, celery, onion, parsley, and salt. Once cooked it is pureed and sieved into a creamy consistency. It can be homemade, but there are many good tomato sauces on the market. Just be sure they don't contain too much spice, as to over-power the dish. (We have found the Hunt-Wesson tomato sauce to be quite right for general purposes.)

TRIPE   Beef tripe, either fresh or frozen, is more readily available than veal tripe and is sold already steam-cleaned and washed.

Tripe should be precooked before its final use by boiling it in lightly salted water, with ¼ cup of vinegar added per quart of water, a small onion, celery stalk, and 2 to 3 whole cloves. Bring to a boil, and cook for 15 minutes. Remove from the heat, drain, and rinse it in fresh water. We repeat the process two or three times (depending on the kind of tripe) until it is tender but still has a bite to it. Once drained and cooled, with a sharp knife trim out any white fatty nodules, and cut the tripe in strips about ¾ × 2½ inches. The tripe is now ready for use. Wrapped in a plastic bag and stored in your refrigerator's meat compartment, it keeps well for a week or so, and nearly forever in the freezer. Generally we purchase, prepare, and store enough tripe for several preparations: When the tripe urge strikes, *la trippa* is there waiting for us.

Broth

Brodo

~

Beef, chicken, fish, and vegetables all make great broths. Beef bones are a great—though not essential—addition to a meat broth, as fish heads and bones are to fish broth. All broths should be started with cold water, and after the first boil, the surface skimmed with a slotted spoon or skimmer to remove all foamy, scummy matter. Once the broth is made, it is strained through a colander or a sieve lined with cheesecloth to retain the solid parts and smaller bits. Further clearing can be done by pouring one or two beaten egg whites into the slow-boiling broth. In cooking they solidify, trapping the broth's smallest floating bits. Once the pot is removed from the heat, the floating egg whites can be skimmed away.

Since making good broth is a lengthy affair, it is good practice to make big batches and then freeze it. Broth freezes well and keeps for months; it should be frozen in four-cup containers, a practical measure for defrosting and using. To use, unmold the frozen broth, place in a pot with a few tablespoons of water, cover, and slowly bring to a boil. Or, if the broth was frozen in a microwave-safe container, defrost it according to your oven's instructions.

Broth can also be frozen in ice cube trays and, when very hard, unmolded, collected in plastic bags, and returned to the freezer.

Canned broth or bouillon cubes may be used in a pinch. Choose a brand, closely inspecting the ingredients used: Avoid those with labels that read like a chemist's shopping list. Use as much canned broth or as many bouillon cubes as necessary to make the equivalent quantity of the broth used in the recipe.

Beef or chicken pieces, once they have made the broth, have given all they've got and have little or no substance left. In Italy they are still considered edible and, diced, either end up in the soup or are used as ingredients for other dishes. If this is the intention from the start, then they are put in the pot once the water and flavoring vegetables are boiling, and then simmered for 1½ to 2 hours, depending on size and type of cut. The resulting broth is somewhat lighter but still very good, especially as a soup base. The meats are scooped out when they are cooked, but not overcooked—probing them with a kitchen fork will tell you.

Beef Broth

Brodo di carne

Beef broth may be made with fresh beef (brisket, bottom round, or soup cuts) and be kept in the refrigerator for three to four days. It also freezes well. This recipe makes approximately 8 cups of broth.

1 to 1½ pounds beef

1 to 2 soup bones

1 celery stalk with leaves

1 carrot, peeled

1 small onion, quartered

2 to 3 plum tomatoes, peeled and crushed, or 2 tablespoons tomato paste

3 quarts cold water, or enough to cover

3 teaspoons salt

2 egg whites (optional)

In a stock pot, combine the beef, bones, celery, carrot, onion, tomatoes, water, and salt. The water should cover the ingredients; if not, add more as necessary. Bring to a boil over medium heat. Scoop off the froth that forms. Cover, reduce the heat, and simmer for about 2½ hours. The meat should be very tender, the broth a light brown color and very flavorful.

Using a sieve lined with cheesecloth, strain the broth into another container. Discard the solids, and allow the liquid to cool. Refrigerate the broth until any fat has congealed on the surface. Scoop off the fat and discard.

To achieve the clearest possible broth, bring the defatted broth to a boil, whisk the two egg whites lightly, stir the whites into the broth, and boil until any remaining particles have been picked up by the egg whites. Remove the pot from the heat, let cool slightly, and scoop out the cooked egg whites. The broth may be used immediately, refrigerated for 3 to 4 days, or frozen in small containers for storage.

Chicken Broth

Brodo di pollo

This recipe yields approximately 8 cups of broth.

In a stock pot, combine the chicken pieces, celery, onion, carrot, tomatoes, peppercorns, water, and salt. Add the water, plus more as necessary to cover. Bring to a boil over medium heat. Scoop off the froth that forms. Cover, reduce the heat, and simmer for about 2½ hours. Let cool a bit and then strain through a sieve lined with cheesecloth into another container. Chill the broth thoroughly and remove any fat that congeals on the surface.

To achieve the clearest possible broth, bring the defatted broth to a boil, whisk the two egg whites lightly, stir the whites into the broth, and boil until any remaining particles have been picked up by the egg whites. Remove the pot from the heat, let cool slightly, and scoop out the cooked egg whites. The broth may be used immediately, refrigerated for 3 to 4 days, or frozen in small containers for storage.

One 3½-pound chicken (or fowl or capon), cut into pieces

1 celery stalk with leaves

1 onion, halved

1 carrot, peeled

3 to 4 plum tomatoes, peeled and crushed, or 2 tablespoons tomato paste

5 peppercorns

3 quarts cold water, or as needed to cover

3 teaspoons salt

2 egg whites (optional)

Vegetable Broth

Brodo di magro

For those who enjoy a nice cup of bouillon without breaking a vegetarian regime, here is a tasty, nicely colored vegetable broth that can be served with a bit of butter and Parmesan cheese. It may be frozen, used as a vegetable base for other soups, or served with small cuts of pasta. This recipe yields approximately 8 cups of broth.

3 quarts cold water

6 medium potatoes, peeled

2 onions, peeled and halved

2 carrots, peeled

2 celery ribs with leaves

4 plum tomatoes, peeled

3 fresh basil leaves

3 sprigs flat-leaf Italian parsley

1 bay leaf

3 teaspoons salt

5 peppercorns

In a stock pot, bring the cold water to a boil. Add the potatoes, onions, carrots, celery, tomatoes, basil, parsley, bay leaf, salt, and peppercorns.

Return the pot to a boil, reduce the heat, cover, and simmer for 2 hours. Add salt to taste.

Strain the broth through a sieve lined with cheesecloth to remove any solids. Use immediately, refrigerate for 3 to 4 days, or freeze for future use.

Fish Broth

Brodo di pesce

As in all fish soups, the more species of fish used for the broth, the better. An absolute requisite is that the fish used be fresh and not of the oily/fatty variety, such as mackerel or bluefish. Most fishmongers save the heads and bones (in the trade, called racks) of the fish that they have fileted. Racks and small whole fish are especially good for making broth. This recipe makes approximately 4 quarts of broth.

In a large stock pot, sauté the garlic and the red pepper pod (if using) in the olive oil until the garlic is golden and the pepper pod is dark brown. Discard the garlic and pepper pod. Add the anchovies and parsley and sauté briefly.

Add the tomatoes and the wine (and the ground red pepper, if using) and cook for 1 minute. Add the fish racks, celery, carrots, bay leaves, onions, and the water, adding more as needed to cover. Bring the mixture slowly to a simmer. Add the salt and simmer, uncovered, for about 1 hour.

Line a large strainer with two thicknesses of cheesecloth and strain the broth into a second container. Use the broth immediately, refrigerate for 3 to 4 days, or freeze for future use.

4 garlic cloves

1 dried cayenne pepper pod, seeded, or ½ teaspoon ground red pepper (optional)

½ cup olive oil

8 anchovy filets, chopped

½ cup chopped fresh flat-leaf Italian parsley

3 cups canned peeled plum tomatoes

2 cups dry white wine

5 pounds fish racks (bones, tails, and heads)

2 celery ribs with leaves

2 carrots, peeled

2 bay leaves

2 medium onions

4 quarts cold water

3 teaspoons salt

Homemade Pasta

Pasta fatta in casa or *Pasta all'uovo*

There are two systems to make homemade pasta—the old and the new. The old system requires more time, more space, more cleanup time, and some practice. The new requires the use of a food processor and a pasta machine, little space, no time at all, and is reasonably clean. In other words, presuming that the food processor is already present in the kitchen, it is well worth investing in the pasta machine (ours is a twenty-five-year-old manual type, still going strong). There are also electric versions of pasta machines, but, at the time of this writing, they are more expensive, noisier, and not much faster than the manual hand-crank versions. The electric kinds that mix, knead, and *extrude* pasta are to be avoided. Only the most sophisticated of experts will know the difference between handmade and machine-made pasta; following are directions for both systems. The measures remain the same: ⅔ cup of flour for each large egg.

1½ *cups all-purpose, unbleached*
flour

½ *teaspoon salt*

2 *large eggs, at room temperature*

FOOD-PROCESSOR PASTA DOUGH

In the bowl of a food processor with the steel blade attached, combine the flour and salt. Pulse to mix.

Beat the eggs in a small bowl, and pour slowly into the running food processor. Process in 4 to 5 three-second bursts for about 1 minute, or until the mixture forms tiny pellets that cling together when pinched. If too small and dry, the pellets will not cling: add slowly 1 to 2 tablespoons of water while processing another few seconds. If the mixture in the processor bowl forms a ball of dough, the mixture is too moist: add 1 to 2 tablespoons of flour while the processor is on until you reach the right consistency. Pour the pellets in a bowl or on a work surface, compress them into a ball of dough, and knead it a few times.

To roll the pasta dough by machine:

Break off a piece of dough as big as the palm of your hand and press it flat. It should not be sticky; if so, dust it with flour. Send it through the widest gap of the machine rollers 4 to 5 times, folding it in half at each pass. When this first stage is completed, the dough should have smoothed out to an almost silky texture.

Reduce the gap width, and send the pasta through. Continue to reduce the gap between the rollers, passing the pasta through the machine until the desired thinness is achieved. (See page 258 for a description of thickness and cuts.)

HANDMADE PASTA DOUGH:

Put the flour and salt in a mound on a lightly floured working surface or large pastry board. Make a well in the center of the mound and crack the eggs into it. With a fork, beat the eggs and stir, picking up flour as you mix. When the developing dough becomes too stiff to stir with a fork and has picked up as much flour as possible, set the fork aside. Flour your hands and begin to knead the dough on the floured surface.

Work in as much of the remaining flour as the dough will take. Knead for 8 to 10 minutes, until you have a smooth and elastic ball of dough.

It should be emphasized that pasta dough, if left to dry too long while still in a ball, can become very hard to manage. Cover the unused dough immediately in plastic wrap.

To roll by hand:

Place the dough in the center of the rolling surface. Flatten it as much as you can with your hands, and begin to roll: place the rolling pin on the center of the dough, and roll it out and away from you, then from the center toward you. Give the dough a 90-degree turn, and roll it again, first from the center away and then from the center toward you. If the dough should stick to the board or pin, sprinkle it very lightly with flour.

Continue turning and rolling the pasta until you have achieved a uniform thickness (about as thick as a dime if making fettuccine, for example).

Once rolled out, the dough may rest on a clean kitchen towel for 10 to 15 minutes, but not so long that the edges become brittle. Cover with second towel or plastic wrap.

To cut pasta by hand:

Fold the pasta up in a flat roll about 4 inches wide. With a very sharp knife, cut the roll in ribbons about ¼-inch wide for fettuccine, as wide as the pasta is thick for tonnarelli (square spaghetti), ¹⁄₁₆-inch wide or thinner for capellini.

When a few slices of pasta have been cut, shake out the ribbons and place them on a floured kitchen towel to dry further. Remember, however, that the longer the pasta dries, the longer it takes to cook.

If making ravioli or similar filled pastas, roll the pasta out to almost paper thin. Cover the pasta with a kitchen towel or plastic wrap until you are ready to add the filling and seal the pasta. Scoop up teaspoons of filling, roll into tiny balls, and place about ½ inch apart on one strip of rolled-out pasta. Cover with a second strip of pasta. With your fingers, press down around the mounds of filling to seal the top pasta to the bottom. Cut in uniform squares with a pastry wheel, or in rounds with a 1½-inch pastry cutter. Place the filled pieces on a flour-dusted cookie sheet.

CAPPELLETTI:

Roll the pasta out to almost paper thin, and cut it into 2 × 2-inch squares. Place a small teaspoon of filling in the center of each square, fold the pasta on the diagonal, and press the edges together tightly to seal, achieving a stuffed triangle.

Wrap the triangle around your finger, one corner over the other, and press to make them stick together. If necessary, moisten the corners where they overlap, and press again. Fold the third corner back on itself, and there is your first cappelletto.

Continue filling and folding until all the squares have been used. Filled pasta may be cooked right away or, after drying out for 30 minutes or so, they may be frozen. Do not defrost frozen cappelletti; instead, plunge them into the boiling liquid while frozen. It will take a minute or two more to cook than fresh cappelletti.

Apulian Homemade Pasta

The pasta used in Apulian soups is made simply with a mixture of hard winter-wheat flour, all-purpose flour, and water. It is reasonably simple to make and it may be used fresh or dried: simply let the cut pasta dry on kitchen towels or place it on a cookie sheet in a warm oven with the door partially open. The recipe below is equivalent to a two-egg batch of pasta.

Combine the semolina flour, all-purpose flour, and the salt in the bowl of a food processor fitted with the cutting blade. Start the machine, and slowly pour in the water, pulsing the machine on and off. Stop adding water as soon as small pellets begin to form; they should stick together when pinched. Depending on the quality of the flour or the humidity of the air, you may need a little more or less water. If a ball of dough forms in the processor, add a little more flour until the ball breaks into pellets. Process on and off a few more times, then pour the pellets onto a work surface. Press them into a ball and knead it a few times. It should be reasonably solid, unsticking dough. Wrap it in a clean kitchen towel or plastic wrap and let it rest for 10 to 15 minutes.

½ cup semolina flour

1 cup all-purpose flour

½ teaspoon salt

¼ cup lukewarm water

To make the dough by hand:

Put the dry ingredients in a bowl, mix with a wooden spoon and slowly add water. Keep mixing and stirring until you have a sort of dough hard to manage with the spoon. Put the dough on a floured surface and knead for 8 or 10 minutes, or until you have a smooth, solid, unsticking ball of dough. Cover and let rest 10 to 15 minutes.

Roll and cut the dough like egg pasta, either by hand or by machine, pages 257–258.

ORECCHIETTE:

Roll a piece of dough into a stick about a finger thick (½ to ¼ inch in diameter). With a sharp knife, cut a thin slice (⅛ inch or less), press your thumb in the center of the slice, and push down and drag the dough on the work surface. It will form a thin, concave shape with thicker edges—the unmistakable shape of a little ear, an orecchietta.

With a little practice, you can roll, cut, press, and drag with the efficiency of a machine!

Another system is to pinch off a chickpea-size bit of dough, press it, and drag it into an orecchietta.

With both systems, no two orecchiette will be the same or will cook exactly to the same point, which adds texture to the dish. They are superior to the machine-made, store-bought kind.

White Bread

Pane bianco

This is a basic recipe for round loaves of homemade white bread, their slices suitable for many soups. It may also be used for making the longer, thinner baguettes which, sliced on the diagonal, can be made into daintier toasts. This recipe yields 2 round loaves or 1 round loaf and 2 baguettes.

Combine the all-purpose flour, whole wheat flour, yeast, and sugar in the bowl of a food processor with its steel blade in place. Pulse to mix.

With the processor on, add the warm water in a steady stream. Continue processing until a dough forms and clumps together at one end of the blade. Turn off the motor, and remove the dough to a floured work surface. The dough should be rather sticky and moist. With floured hands, knead rapidly for about 7 minutes, or until the dough is very elastic and soft. Let rest for 5 minutes.

Put the olive oil in a large 3½-quart bowl. Place the dough in the bowl, turning the dough to coat all the surfaces of the bowl and dough with the oil.

Cover the bowl with plastic wrap, leaving it open on each side. Place a well-wrung-out dishtowel, dampened in hot water, over the plastic wrap.

Let the dough rise in a draft-free place (an unheated oven works well in winter, or on the countertop in summer) for at least 1 hour, or until the dough has tripled in size.

Preheat the oven to 425°F.

5¾ cups all-purpose unbleached flour, plus more as needed

¼ cup whole wheat flour

2 envelopes (2 tablespoons) "rapid rise" yeast

1 teaspoon sugar

2 cups warm (120 to 130°F) water

1½ teaspoons salt

1½ tablespoons olive oil

Butter

2 to 3 tablespoons cornmeal

Butter the bread pans, and dust them with cornmeal.

Remove the towel and plastic wrap, and turn the dough out onto a floured surface. Punch down the dough, sprinkle with the salt, and knead briefly. Shape the dough into the loaves desired, and place in the bread pans.

Bake for 15 minutes, then reduce the heat to 375°F. Spray the loaves with a mist of water (we use a spray bottle). Bake for another 30 minutes, spraying again after 15 minutes. The bread is done when the loaves sound hollow when tapped on the underside with your knuckles. Allow the bread to cool before slicing.

Whole Wheat Bread

Pane integrale

This recipe yields 2 round loaves or 1 round loaf and 2 baguettes.

1¼ cups all-purpose unbleached white flour, plus more as needed

2 cups stone-ground whole wheat flour

2 envelopes (2 tablespoons) "rapid rise" yeast

2 teaspoons sugar

2 cups warm (120 to 130°F) water

Combine the white flour, whole wheat flour, yeast, and the sugar in the bowl of a food processor with its steel blade in place. Pulse until mixed.

With the processor on, add the warm water in a steady stream. Continue processing until a ball of dough forms at one end of the blade. Turn off the motor, and remove the dough to a floured work surface. The dough should be rather moist and sticky.

With floured hands, knead rapidly for 5 to 7 minutes, until the dough is very elastic and soft. Let rest for 10 minutes.

Put the olive oil in a large 3½-quart bowl. Place the dough in the bowl, turning the dough to coat all the surfaces of the bowl and dough with the oil.

Cover the bowl with plastic wrap, leaving it open on each side. Place a well-wrung-out dishtowel, dampened in hot water, over the plastic wrap.

Let the dough rise in a draft-free place (an unheated oven in the winter, or on a countertop in the summer) for 2 hours, or until the dough has nearly tripled in size.

Remove the towel and plastic wrap, and turn the dough out onto a floured surface. Punch down the dough, sprinkle with the salt, and knead briefly. Shape the dough into the loaves desired. Tuck in the outer edge of the round(s) or ends of the baguettes. Butter the bread pans very lightly, and sprinkle with the cornmeal.

Preheat the oven to 375°F.

Place the shaped loaves in the pans, and let them rise for 10 to 15 minutes. Bake for about 50 minutes. Spray the loaves lightly with a mist of water (we use a spray bottle) after 10 minutes, and again after 20 minutes of baking time.

When you estimate the bread is done, lift it off the tin and tap the underside with your knuckles. If the bread sounds hollow, it is done. Allow to cool before slicing.

2 teaspoons salt

1½ tablespoons olive oil

Butter

2 to 3 tablespoons cornmeal

Sardinian Music-Paper Bread

Carta da musica

Carta da musica is a unique Sardinian bread. Because of its long-lasting qualities, it was prepared for shepherds to carry on their long stays at winter or summer pastures. The name derives from its paper-thin, parchment-like texture and the singed scores left by griddle or grill.

Carta da musica is made with white Italian bread dough, rolled very thin; it takes some practice but is not particularly difficult to make at home. The real item should be baked in a wood-fired oven to assure hot, constant, dry heat.

A close alternative to *carta da musica* is pita bread, or pocket bread, once available only in Middle Eastern specialty stores, but now readily available in most markets.

When using pita, place the round bread in a 300°F oven for a few minutes to make it easier to separate the bread's top and bottom layers. Then, while still warm, peel the two layers apart, and return them to the oven to toast until barely golden and crisp. To obtain the singed markings, the same procedure can be done on a hot grill or griddle. Watch carefully, though—it is easy to overdo it.

3 cups all-purpose flour, plus more as needed

1 envelope (1 tablespoon) "rapid rise" yeast

½ teaspoon salt

1 cup warm (120° to 130°F) water

Olive oil

Combine the flour, yeast, and salt in the bowl of a food processor with its steel blade in place. With the machine running, slowly pour in the warm water until a ball of dough forms. (If too dry, add a few drops of water; if too wet, add a pinch or two of flour.) When the ball forms, let the machine run for another 15 seconds.

Transfer the dough to a lightly floured work surface and knead it briefly. Place the dough in a lightly oiled bowl, cover, and let it rise in a warm place for about 1 hour.

Preheat the oven to 450°F.

Knead the dough again for 1 minute. Divide it into 3-inch balls, and roll them into rounds, approximately 12 inches in diameter. Roll the rounds as thin as you can make them, dusting with flour as necessary.

Place the rounds on cookie sheets, and bake, watching carefully. Retrieve the rounds as soon as they start to blow up and blister. While still warm and soft, separate the two layers of the blistered rounds and allow to cool.

Reduce the heat to 300°F. Toast the separated rounds until they are barely golden. Serve warm, either whole or broken into large chips.

Served warm or cold, beware: *Carta da musica* is addictive!

Index

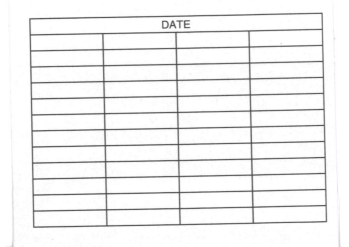

DATE